I0879421

The Siege of Sziget

Miklós Zrínyi

The Siege of Sziget

Translated by László Kőrössy

With an introduction by George Gömöri

The Catholic University of America Press
Washington, D. C.

The paper used in this publication meets the minimum requirements of American National Standards for Information Science—Permanence of Paper for Printed Library Materials, ANSI Z39.48-1984.
∞

Library of Congress Cataloging-in-Publication Data
Zrínyi, Miklós, graf, 1620–1664.
[Szigeti veszedelem. English]
The siege of Sziget / Miklós Zrínyi ; translated by László Korössy ; with an introduction by George Gömöri.
p. cm.
Includes bibliographical references.
ISBN 978-0-8132-1861-8 (pbk. : alk. paper) 1. Hungarian poetry Translations into English. I. Korössy, László, 1986– II. Gömöri, George, 1934– III. Title.
PH3194.Z8S9 2011
894'.51111—dc22 2011000129

for Maria

CONTENTS

Translator's Acknowledgments ix
Introduction *by George Gömöri* xi
Note on Translation xxv

The Siege of Sziget

PREFACE 3
PART ONE 7
PART TWO 24
PART THREE 38
PART FOUR 56
PART FIVE 72
PART SIX 87
PART SEVEN 105
PART EIGHT 122
PART NINE 137
PART TEN 153
PART ELEVEN 170
PART TWELVE 185
PART THIRTEEN 202
PART FOURTEEN 217
PART FIFTEEN 236
POSTSCRIPT 253

Epigrams 255
Glossary 257
List of Characters 259
Bibliography *by Steven Béla Várdy* 263

TRANSLATOR'S ACKNOWLEDGMENTS

This work was accomplished solely by the grace of God.

I would like to thank, first of all, my wife, my inspiration.

I must also thank my mother, who gave me my language, and whose challenge was the genesis of this project; my father, who has been for me the model of a true patriot; and my grandmother, whose love will always impact every part of my life. Their reflections will be glimpsed in these pages. I thank Alex Bender for his unfailing loyalty and friendship, which has seen me through this and countless other adventures. I thank Drs. Leonora Neville and David McGonagle, without whose kindness and wisdom this manuscript would, simply, not have been published. I was led to this particular publisher because of my blessed experience at the Catholic University of America, an experience built and enriched by so many: Drs. Laura Mayhall and John Kromkowski; Drs. Kevin White, James O'Leary, and Stephen Schneck; Frs. O'Connell and Schlageter; and most especially Drs. Ingrid Merkel and Jerry Muller. I want to thank also all the friends and family members whose support and camaraderie also shaped this work: Zoli, Árpád, Kati, Dave, the Anthonys, Ryan, Jenn, Rob, Regan, Elise, Miss Willie, and the Coloradans. And finally, I must thank my families, who have shaped and guided me, in Maryland, Connecticut, Hungary, and elsewhere.

I am indebted to Dr. Béla Várdy and George Gömöri, who elevated this manuscript from a mere translation to a work of scholarly esteem and importance; and to Dr. Peter Sherwood for his bottomless kindness and support.

My fervent wish is that I will have "written it as it was," and that my project would have met with the approval of Count Miklós Zrínyi, who I thank, finally, for his gift to me.

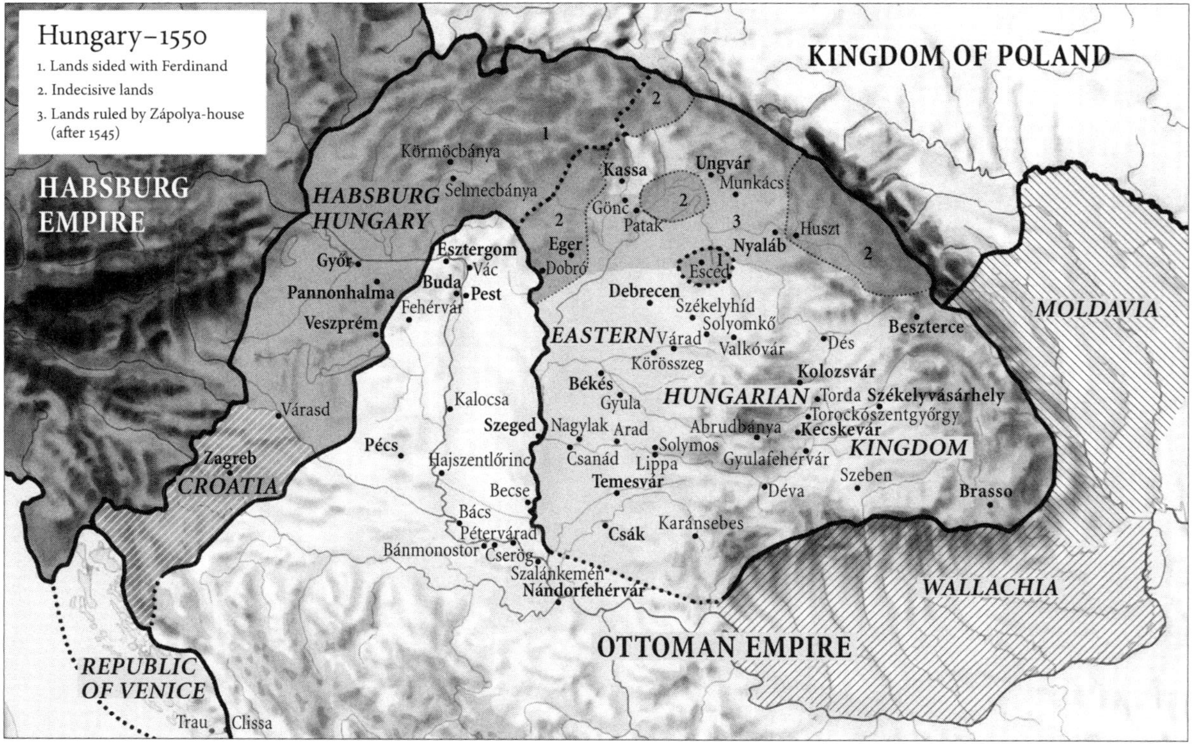

Hungary c. 1550 (sixteen years before the siege of Sziget), with Habsburg, Ottoman, and independent territories. Szigetvár is 30 km west of Pécs, in the Ottoman-occupied zone.

INTRODUCTION

George Gömöri

Count Nicholas Zríni (in modern Hungarian Miklós Zrínyi), author of *The Siege of Sziget,* was deliberately given the same Christian name as his distinguished sixteenth-century great-grandfather, known to Hungarian historians as Miklós Zrínyi of Szigetvár or Zríni, bán of Croatia. This great-grandfather, who is the central figure of the epic poem, was the heroic defender of the castle of Szigetvár in 1566, eighty years prior to the work. To avoid confusion I shall refer to the author of *The Siege of Sziget* as Count Miklós Zrínyi and to his great-grandfather as Bán Miklós Zríni. To understand the importance of the defense of Szigetvár it is necessary to look at it within the context of Hungary's struggle against the Ottoman Turks, which had begun centuries earlier and was still ongoing during the time the poem was written.

In 1526, forty years before the narrative of the poem, a decisive battle took place near Mohács, a town in southern Hungary, marking the end of the medieval kingdom of Hungary. Louis II, Hungary's young Jagiello king, died during the battle, along with many members of the nobility, the remainder of which split into two groups, one accepting the claim of the Habsburg king, Ferdinand I, to the throne of Hungary, the other group electing as king the Hungarian-born János Zápolya.[1] This split enabled Suleyman, the sultan of the Ottoman Empire, to make an alliance with Zápolya against the Habsburgs, allowing him three years later in 1529 to cross the country and launch an unsuccessful attack on Vienna.

1. The Jagiellos were a large multinational dynasty, founded by King Wladyslaw II Jagiello of Poland (1362–1434).

The nobility supported in turn either the Habsburgs or Zápolya, but by 1538, after much infighting, it became clear that neither king could establish absolute rule in Hungary. Ferdinand and Zápolya finally came to an agreement by which Ferdinand recognized Zápolya as king of Hungary, while the latter promised him the throne after his death, even were he to have an heir.

Zápolya married in 1539, producing a son, John Sigismund, but died within a year. Ferdinand, backed by a faction of the Hungarian nobility, made his claim to be sole ruler of the land by trying to occupy Buda. However, Zápolya's followers proclaimed the baby John Sigismund king of Hungary, with the support of Suleyman, who arrived with a huge army, ostensibly to protect the infant king and Isabella, his mother. What Suleyman in fact did do was to capture and occupy Buda and banish Isabella and the infant king to Transylvania. This action created three separate territories: Transylvania, ruled by a governor representing the infant king; western and northern Hungary, remaining under Habsburg rule; and Buda and central Hungary, now under the rule of Suleyman. After continued fighting over territory between the Habsburgs and the Turks, an armistice was reached in 1547, in which it was agreed that Ferdinand would pay an annual tribute of thirty thousand gold florins to the sultan.

The armistice lasted only four years, after which time the Turks once again attempted to increase their territories at the expense of the Habsburgs. They took several fortresses, with campaigns throughout the 1550s up to the time of Ferdinand's death in 1564. Ferdinand's successor, Maximilian II, stopped the payment of annual tribute money to the Turks and a year later attacked Transylvania, still under Turkish protection.

This resulted in the Turks taking up arms once again, with the ultimate aim of capturing Vienna. We finally come to Sziget or Szigetvár, the captain of which at this time is the hero of the poem, Bán Miklós Zríni. Sziget was a recently fortified castle north of the river Drave, which by its geographical position was regarded as the "gateway to Vienna." Suleyman reached Sziget and attacked it in August 1566: this episode is the central theme of Count Miklós Zrínyi's epic poem.

The great-grandfather, Bán Miklós Zríni (born in 1508), the captain of Szigetvár, with several thousand Croatian and Hungarian soldiers held out against the Turks for over a month. (Of Croatian origin, Zríni nevertheless identified with the Hungarian nobility and had fought bravely at the previous Turkish siege of Vienna. He was Bán of Croatia between 1542 and 1556, becoming captain of Sziget in 1561.) He held out against the Turks for several weeks in the mistaken hope that relief would eventually arrive. The imperial army, however, was some distance away, in upper Hungary; its commanders prevaricated, and consequently after the brave resistance, Sziget fell to the Turks, with almost all its defenders including Bán Zríni dying in the final attack.

The most reliable historian of the time, Ferenc Forgách, suggests that Bán Zríni was a rather unscrupulous, headstrong, temperamental person, and some of his arbitrary actions earned him the name of "robber baron." Nevertheless, he redeemed himself through his heroic defense of Sziget, which ended with the sacrifice of his own life.

Just like his valiant ancestor, Count Miklós Zrínyi (1620–1664) too was predestined to fight the Ottoman Turks who still occupied a greater part of Hungary in his own lifetime. Known abroad as an outstanding military commander under the name "Serini" (or in some Venetian sources even "Sdrini"), few readers of contemporary European newsletters suspected that he also wrote both poetry and political tracts, or indeed that he started his career simultaneously as both soldier and poet.

"Serinimania," the cult of the latter Zrínyi, reached its highest point in London in the summer of 1664. Interest in him had been growing for some time, and was heightened at the time of the publication of a 168-page book by Samuel Speed, entitled *The Conduct and Character of Count Nicholas Serini, Protestant Generalissimo of the Auxiliaries of Hungary.* (This title contained an error: Count

Zrínyi was in fact Catholic, though a very tolerant one.) The preface to this collection was signed with the initials O.C., an editor unidentified to this day. During the same time there was an advertisement in a London newsletter stating that an image, the "true Pourtraiture" of the "Noble Count Nicholas Serini . . . presented to the Kings most Excellent Majesty" could be purchased from a certain bookshop "next door to the Signe of the Drake without Temple-Barre." This image was the same one that William Faithorne Jr., a fashionable engraver of the period, made of Count Miklós Zrínyi. In the second half of the book Zrínyi's role in the Turkish war of 1663–1664 is compared to two earlier great opponents of the Turks, that is, "Tamberlain" and Scanderbeg, and he is praised as "the great Champion of Christendome" upon whom "the eyes of Europe" are fixed.[2] His minor victories, including those in the "Winter campaign" being continuously reported, raised his profile and were a welcome antidote to the shock felt by all of Christian Europe over the earlier loss of the key fortress Érsekujvár (Neuhausel) in northern Hungary, which brought the Turks within striking distance of Vienna.

Although he did not claim a share in the decisive victory of St. Gotthard (an event that was even noted in Pepys's diary), the cult of Count Miklós Zrínyi in England outlasted his death, which took place during a boar hunt in November 1664. Soon afterward a small funerary anthology, *Lacrymae Europae,* edited by Pál P. Jászberényi, a Hungarian expatriate, was printed in London. It contained poems in Latin by three Hungarians including the editor, all of whom resided in London at the time; a Swedish mathematician, Johannes Megalinus (also living in London); an Austrian priest; and a German-Polish historian, Joachim Pastorius. The editor Pál P. Jászberényi was a succesful Latin master, maintaining a private school at Charing Cross which was immensely popular in Charles II's London. In Paris, Jean Loret, author of a printed

2. Tamur Lenk or Tamerlane (1336–1405) was a central Asian warlord who tried to restore Mongol supremacy; his descendants founded India's Mughal dynasty; Gjergj Kastrioti Scanderbeg (1405–1468), was an Albanian war leader who successfully opposed the Ottoman invasion of his country.

journal in verse, also mourned the valiant Count Miklós Zrínyi, extolling him in the highest terms, saying that he was a hero of such stature that he could easily have been taken for "a Frenchman of quality."

Though *The Siege of Sziget* was published in Vienna thirteen years prior to his death, during his lifetime Count Miklós Zrínyi was praised throughout Europe only for his military career and for his wise statesmanship, not for his literary achievements, interest in which began only in the nineteenth century. Even in Hungary itself little attention was paid to his book of poems, *Adriai tengernek Syrenaia* (Siren of the Adriatic Sea), when it was published in Vienna in 1651. It was this collection which contained several lyrical pieces as well as the epic poem *Obsidionis Sigetianae Libri XV,* known later as *Szigeti veszedelem* (The Siege of Sziget), which was written between 1645 and 1648 and is the story of Bán Miklós Zríni, Count Miklós Zrínyi's great-grandfather, and his heroic defense of the fortress of Sziget in 1566. This work is the first Hungarian epic poem of importance of the Central European baroque.

News of the defense of Sziget and the death of Bán Miklós Zríni resonated throughout sixteenth-century Europe. While the fortress of Sziget was eventually taken by the Turkish army led by Suleyman the Magnificent, it was a Pyrrhic victory, because the sultan himself died two days prior to the final assault on the castle. Despite the fact that the fortress of Sziget fell, the Turks were stopped in their tracks from making further advances, thereby giving rise to a potent Christian legend comparable only to that of the naval victory over the Turks at Lepanto some years later. Bán Miklós Zríni retained the respect of his enemies even after he died. The basha of Buda sent the fallen hero's head preserved in wine and vinegar to the camp of the Imperial Army. In a poem written many years later, Paul Melissus-Schede, a neo-Latin poet, recalls that the Emperor Maximillian being there present, burst into tears upon seeing the severed head of Bán Zríni, whom he was unwilling or unable to assist in the defense of Sziget.

Apart from a number of contemporary accounts, for instance,

that of the Croatian Francisco Crnko (which became well known in Europe in Samuel Budina's Latin translation), the 1566 fall of Sziget was also documented in early Italian and German writings, such as the anonymous *Historia di Zigeth, ispugnata da Suliman Re de' Turchi* (Venice, 1570). It is also described in Latin histories, for instance, in Pietro Bizarri's *Pannonicum Bellum* (Basle, 1573), and in the multinational poetic anthology *De Sigetho Hungariae propugnacolo* (Wittenberg, 1587). In all these writings Szigetvár is hailed as an important bulwark of Christianity. Its defense also figured prominently in the most popular Turkish history of the seventeenth century, Richard Knolles's *The generall historie of the Turkes,* wherein the 1610 folio edition under the picture of Suleyman the Magnificent the historian Phillip Lonicer's original Latin poem is translated as follows:

His fathers Empire *Solyman* doth rule with mightie power,
And Christian kingdoms ceaseth not with slaughter to devour.
The auncient Rhodes, with NAXOS isle, and PAROS he did take,
And on the coast of ITALIE did wofull havocke make.
Faire Hungarie with armies great he often did annoy,
And with a world of men had thought Vienna to destroy.
But whilest to *Sigeth* he laied siege, in hope the same to have,
Cut off by death in his great pride, went naked to his grave.

Knolles devotes three folio pages to Sziget's defense, beginning with the sentence: "In this town was Governour *Nicholaus Serinius*...a valiant man, and a mortall enemy of the Turks, with a Garrison of 2300 good souldiors" and ends his narrative with Bán Miklós Zríni's severed head being sent to the emperor's camp and finally laid to rest at Csáktornya (Tschakaturn).

There were several earlier treatments on the subject of the defense of Sziget, some of which must have been known to Count Miklós Zrínyi, such as the twenty-page-long poem in Croatian, *Vazetje Sigeta grada,* by Brne Karnarutic (Venice, 1584). Knowing Italian, he must also have read Tasso's *Gerusalemme liberata* and Marino's shorter epic poems *(Del Strage degli Innocenti; Gerusal-*

emme distrutta) which he emulated in his ambitious attempt to celebrate the Hungarian and Croatian Christian defenders of Sziget Castle. Clearly, Miklós Zrínyi's work was written in order to raise the national awareness and identity of the Hungarian nation as well as that of the Croatians, who were in alliance with Habsburg-ruled Hungary against the Turks.

Apart from the Italian models Zrínyi the poet also looked back to antiquity. His collection *Adriai tengernek Syrenaja* shows the strong impact of Virgil, popular in Hungary already in the sixteenth century, and indeed Virgil can be identified as one of Count Miklós Zrínyi's main poetic models. The opening line of the *Aeneid,* "Arma virumque cano…" is replicated in the *invocatio* of Zrínyi's epic in the following lines:

> I, who once with youthful mind
> Played with love's sweet verse
> .....
> Now with Mars's greater poetry
> Arms and heroes I sing!

In his preface to *The Siege of Sziget* Count Zrínyi also compares himself to Virgil, who he says worked on his epic for ten years, while he needed only a year to complete his own poem! Whether this really is true or not, throughout his entire life Count Miklós successfully played a dual role, appearing both as poet and author of political tracts and as an outstanding military commander succesfully fighting the Turks. In this poem he demonstrates his impresssive talent as a poet, as well as his thorough understanding of military tactics and technique.

❧

The Siege of Sziget is based on the idea that God has sent the Ottoman Turks to punish Hungarians for their sins, that is, for their un-Christian, sybaritic way of life. According to the poet, this punishment can be revoked if the Hungarians repent, an idea first formulated by sixteenth-century Protestant preachers. The epic begins with the Turks already occupying a large part of

Hungary and planning further attacks on Hungarian fortresses, including that of Sziget, led by Sultan Suleyman. This fortress, though, is commanded and defended by soldiers who have retained their Christian beliefs and who embody the best virtues of both the Hungarian and the Croatian nations. Though the Turkish army suffers huge losses, the army's unity being shattered after the death of the sultan, the castle is finally taken. Despite this apparent victory, it is a hollow one, as the heroic defense of Sziget became a symbol of Christian resistance, remaining so almost a century later, when the poem was written and Count Nicholas Zrínyi was still fighting the Turks and right up to the time that the Turks were finally driven out of Hungary.

In this sense the poem *The Siege of Sziget* is a *symbolic beginning of the end* for the Ottoman Empire. Like Tasso's *Gerusalemme liberata,* in which the author calls for the liberation of Turkish-occupied Greece, *The Siege of Sziget* too is a clarion call not just for defending Hungary against the Turks, but to become proactive and carry the war into Turkish-occupied territory. (This indeed is what Count Zrínyi himself did twelve years after the publication of the poem in the winter campaign of 1663–1664.)

Count Zrínyi's poem is a typical product of the baroque in several respects, for example, by making use of a metaphysical apparatus. This is a method used also by Tasso in his above-mentioned grand epic. God sends the Archangel Gabriel to Godfrey de Boullion to plant in his mind the idea of a crusade for the liberation of Jerusalem. In *The Siege of Sziget,* God, wanting to punish the Hungarians, sends the Archangel Michael to hell, in order to unchain the Fury Alecto, so that she can prompt Suleyman to launch a campaign against the sinning Hungarians. Like Tasso who mobilizes a host of Furies against the Christians later in his work, Zrínyi too uses the metaphysical ploy of hellish demons raised by the demon Alecto's black magic to be used as auxiliaries of the Turkish army during the final storming of Sziget. Another supernatural element is Alecto appearing in the sultan's dream in the guise of Selim, his father, urging the sultan to take action: "Get up, gird a sharp sword to your side, / Go with your armies upon the erring Magyars" (1.38). This is an ancient topos, first introduced by Herodotus (the ghost of the Persian shah's father urging him to go into war against the Greeks) whom Zrínyi knew either in a Latin translation or through some later secondary source. The idea, however, that the fight of the Turks with the Christians is accompanied by a struggle between divine forces ("the gods") is even older—it goes back to Homer's *Iliad* where individual heroes are often protected in battle by their supernatural mothers or most respected god-sponsor from Olympus.

The Siege of Sziget is nevertheless quite different from Tasso in one important respect. Tasso chose his theme from the eleventh century, an age distant enough to have become part history, part legend. While he was a technically consummate poet, he had never served in a proper war, he had never "tasted blood." Count Miklós Zrínyi, on the other hand, was, in Antal Szerb's words "someone... who is an epic hero himself." His experience of warfare is not bookish, but very real; in fact, he wrote his epic poem during a pause between two military campaigns. Thanks to this, he was in a unique position and because the relatively short time-gap between the poem's "narrative time" and its actual writing—just about eighty years—the military situation in Turkish-occupied Hungary did not change much. The Turks were still trying to break through the defense line of fortresses to advance on Vienna and in spite of periodic truces Turkish or Turkish-allied Tartar incursions were still endangering the lives of the population in that northern and western sliver of territory which remained of the original Kingdom of Hungary. Castles like Kanizsa or Székesfehérvár (Alba Regalis) were still hotly contested—with one difference: by that time the Turks resident in Hungary knew their indigenous foes much better and the Hungarians had also learned to respect the military virtues of their arch-enemy.

This is why in Zrínyi's epic the representation of the Turks is more subtle, or if you like, more complex than in any previous Hungarian literary work. The merits of the "clever," though tyrannical, Suleyman the Magnificent are extolled by the poet and the martial talents of individual Turks and their allies are also clearly recognized. This seems to be necessary for the structure of the poem—the contest between Deli Vid, an outstanding Croatian fighter from Sziget and brave Demirham would not be possible without showing that the Turkish army has not only incompetent leaders and drug addicts (like Basha Arslan) but also people with a serious commitment to the green banner of the prophet Mohammed.[3] All this does not change the fact that—as most Hungarian chroniclers ascertain—on the whole Turkish promises cannot be trusted and that in Zrínyi's eyes Christianity is superior to Islam, God being firmly on the side of the Christians even when meting out punishment for "their sins." Even the evil magician Alderan realizes toward the end of the epic that in spite of the fall of the castle "with the Christians stands the true God" (14.67).

The plot itself is slow to unfold in *The Siege of Sziget.* It starts in heaven with God's decision to send out the archangel Michael, and continues with Basha Arslan's ill-fated attack on the fortress of Palota and Bán Zríni's prayer in the chapel of the castle of Szigetvár. Up to Arslan's setback at Palota the Turkish army seems to ignore Zríni's castle, but after his victory at Siklós he draws upon himself the wrath of the sultan. So the poem is really constructed in two parts: after all the preliminaries the real siege of Sziget begins only in Part Seven. While according to historians the Turks led several assaults on the castle (Istvánffy in his chronicle claims that there were ten attacks) Zrínyi, the poet, compresses all into one major assault in Part Ten—which is unsuccessful because of the heroic resistance of the defenders. While the numerical superiority of Suleyman's army is stressed, most Christian defenders of the castle are described as dedicated fighters and their steadfastness can be broken only by a host of demonic forces.

When Hungarian critics such as Tibor Klaniczay speak about

3. Duels between Hungarian and Turkish fighters witnessed by their respective troops took place already in the sixteenth century. One of these, between György Kapitán and Aga Hubiar, took place in 1550 and was recorded by a Hungarian lutanist-poet, *Tinódi Lantos.* See *Sebestyén válogatott munkái* (Budapest, 1956), 127–35.

"baroque realism" in *The Siege of Sziget,* they have in mind the realistic description of warfare and actual fighting, with individuated (named) characters on both sides. Although they are only episodic characters, on the Christian side Radovan and Juranić are clearly delineated; in the camp of the Turks Demirham and Rustan similarly appear vividly. This microrealism does not exclude real pathos or eliminate a tendency to idealize or monumentalize specific moments of the battle. Visionary elements are also present—for example, Zrínyi's prayer in Part Three, where the cross on the altar bends down three times and he is "addressed" from heaven about the fate of Sziget. An all-important dramatic moment is construed at the end of the epic when the bán of Croatia falls in the battle only *after* he killed the sultan himself! This event, contradicted by the most reliable chroniclers of the siege, was nonetheless necessary in order to present a *symbolic victory* of Bán Zrínyi and his Christian soldiers over the followers of Mohammed. When the bán himself is overwhelmed by Turkish swords and bullets, the metaphysical theater reaches its grand finale: Zrínyi is miraculously "saved," that is, lifted into heaven by a special detachment of angels (14.107):

> The angelic legions immediately descends
> Glorify God with ringing music.
> Gabriel with twice ten others, the bán's soul
> Lifts from the ground on splendid wings.

This is a scene that could have been painted by Tintoretto or another great painter of the early baroque.

That the poet is not entirely faithful to historical facts is clearly stated in the preface: "I have blended my history with legends," though admittedly, the word used by Count Zrínyi, *fabula,* can be translated differently, meaning "fables" or "made-up stories." "Fabulas" indeed abound in *The Siege of Sziget,* to name a few the repeated duels between Deli Vid and Demirham belong to this category, as well as the story of "love-mad" Deliman and the sultan's daughter, the beautiful Cumilla. One could ask why is it that the only real love story occurs on the Turkish side? Christian heroes seem to hide their personal feelings, dedicating all their energy to exercise and actual fighting. The main hero himself has no time for his family—in fact, as soon as he realizes that the main Turkish thrust is against Sziget, he sends away his son György to safety, with a letter asking for help from the emperor. Whatever happens, young György has to survive, to bear witness, telling his father's story to the world.

Already the poet János Arany pointed out the beauty of the lyrical episodes in Zrínyi's epic. Perhaps the most beautiful of these is in the first few stanzas of part eight in which "graceful red dawn" flies in "on winged horse" while "its bridle washes in white foam." This lyrical mood changes, however, with Dawn arriving at Sziget and seeing a multitude of rotting corpses near the walls of the castle. Another charming lyrical inset is the song of the handsome Turkish boy, a servant of Basha Mehmet who accompanies himself on the *kobza,* a winged instrument. The young page sings a praise of fortune, basically his own good fortune which allows him to live in comfort, enjoying the beauty of each season. This song on fortune (3.32–39) is answered indirectly by the poet himself after the death of Basha Mehmet in the opening stanzas of part four, in a sense "correcting" the song of the Turkish page:

> Fortune delights in man's fall
> So she lifts him up, placing him even in the heavens
> . . . . .
> Happy is who is less conceited
> But with a ready heart awaits Fortune's whirling.

The original figure, Fortuna, is a blind goddess and as such she can be very capricious. It is not hard to detect stoicism in the lines quoted above and of course one is immediately reminded of Zrínyi's often-quoted motto: "Sors bona nihil aliud" (Good fortune, nothing else). In warfare, as well as in the good husbanding of one's talents, what is needed is fortune above all.

The language of *The Siege of Sziget* is innovative at least in one respect. While Turkish words occasionally occur in the so-called Hungarian historical songs *(históriás ének)* of the sixteenth century, Zrínyi deliberately uses them (as well as Croat and Latin words) in several instances, either to add "colour locale" to his verse or just to "enrich" his poetic language. This he justifies with the excuse that "the Hungarian language is impoverished," a conclusion which he reached after reading histories in Latin and Italian. At the same time, a recent history and catalogue of his library shows that he used several sources in Hungarian, such as Gáspár Heltai's *Chronica az magyaroknac dolgairol* (Kolozsvár, 1575), which he called the "Hungarian Bonfini" and often wrote Hungarian glosses in the margins of his books.[4] Although there is no trace of it in his library catalogue, it is probable that Zrínyi also had access to *Cancionale,* a collection of "historical songs" published by the same printer/publisher Heltai which contained detailed descriptions in verse of both succesful and unsuccesful Turkish sieges of Hungarian castles in the sixteenth century. The influence of these poems on Zrínyi can be detected in the swearing speech made by the 1566 captain of Sziget where among other things he warns against believing in Turkish promises, as "Foolish is he who gives Turks' words his trust, / For with his castle, he loses his life" (5.29) referring to the case of István Losonci, captain of Temesvár, who paid for trusting the Turks "with his precious life."[5] Although the odds are stacked against the defenders, Bán Zríni makes them swear to hold out to the bitter end with these words: "Let this place and this fortress be our glory, / Or vultures' bellies be our tombs" (4.34).

The Siege of Sziget is written in rhyming quatrains, in a twelve-syllable line which can be defined as a "Hungarian alexandrine." Much has been written about the alleged irregularity of his line, for Zrínyi did not keep to the 6-6 syllable caesura but varied his line according to the exigencies of the subject, producing either

4. Tibor Klaniczay, ed., *A Bibliotheca Zriniana története és állománya* (Budapest, 1991).

5. Zrínyi uses the older form "Tömösvár" (today Timisoara in Romania). Losonci's story is also included in Heltai's *Cancionale* (1574).

7-5 or 5-7 caesuras in different lines. Modern critics point out that while some other Hungarian poets of the same age write perfect alexandrines that makes the stanza rather monotonous, Zrínyi's decision to ignore this rule was deliberate. A more flexible line can reproduce speeches and emotional statements better and Zrínyi uses this technique to good effect. In other words, he is as accomplished a poet as any of his less traveled and more "professional" contemporaries.

He was also aware of his literary achievement. In an age when kings and popes (James I or Urban VIII) wrote verse and emperors (like Leopold I of Austria) composed music, he wrote a great Christian epic poem which had not existed before him in Hungarian and which—due to the Croatian translation by his brother, Peter, in 1660—became an epic of defining importance for the Croatian nation.[6] It can be claimed without exaggeration that in spite of the lack of instant recognition *The Siege of Sziget* belongs to the best epics of the European baroque, making a huge impact on Hungarian poets as late as the nineteenth century. As this great poet and military commander wrote it in a spirit of Horatian self-esteem in the "Postscript" *(Bérekesztés)* to his work:

> Here I have brought my work to a close,
> Which jealous time, nor water can wash away,
> Nor the heavens' thunder, nor iron can ruin,
> Nor that great enemy, jealousy can harm.

In the third stanza of this poem Miklós Zrínyi speaks of the "fame and respect" which he expects from the world for his person and his literary work. May the present translation by László Kőrössy be a major step toward gaining universal fame for a grand Christian epic written in Hungarian almost three hundred and fifty years ago.

6. *Adrianszkoga mora Syrena Groff Zrinski Petar* (Venice, 1660).

NOTE ON TRANSLATION

The most common title for Zrínyi's work is *Szigeti veszedelem,* Hungarian that translates to the "Peril of Sziget." However, this is a later innovation, and the author's original title was Latin, *Obsidionis szigetianae,* meaning instead the "Siege of Sziget." For the sake of accuracy, the Latin title was chosen to be retained, rather than the more familiar Hungarian one.

The reader may notice that Sziget and Szigetvár are used interchangeably throughout the text; *sziget* is the Hungarian word for "island," while *vár* is the word for "fort" or "fortress," so while the name of the town and fortress is officially Szigetvár, Sziget is a common abbreviation.

In Hungarian literature generally, and in poetry particularly, it is considered proper form to change tenses regularly; this can be used to heighten excitement or to achieve poetic effect. This may at first be somewhat disconcerting to the reader, but it is no mistake.

In Hungarian, the family name precedes the given name, and this order has been retained in the translation. The spelling of Turkish names has been changed to agree with modern English standards.

The Siege of Sziget

PREFACE

To the Reader:

Homer wrote his history one hundred years after the peril of Troy; it so happened that I should also write my history one hundred after the peril of Sziget. Virgil wrote the Aeneid over ten years; it so happened that it took me one year, that is, one winter, to bring my work to completion. I compare my pen to neither, but I may boast before them that my profession and vocation is not poetry, but rather is greater and more useful in the service of our nation:[1] that which I have written, I have written as a diversion; I seek nothing by it. They had no other tasks; this was the least of my tasks. I wrote as I could, though in a few places I could have written better, had I not spent my time in other pursuits. There are deficiencies in my verses, but there are in the moon and in the sun as well, those which we call eclipses. If they say: *saepe et magnus dormitat Homerus,*[2] then indeed without shame I may examine my flaws, for I say truly, I have not once proofread my work, for I had not time, and so it is the firstborn of my mind. And even were I to proofread it, still it would not be *in perfectione, quia nihil perfectum sub Sole, nam nec chorda sonum dat, quem vult manus et mens.*[3] I have blended my history with legends, but so I have learned from Homer and Virgil; he who has read these may distinguish one from the other. Turkish, Croat, Latin words I have mixed into my verses, for I thought it more pleasing thus, and then

1. Zrínyi was a general in the Austrian/Hungarian/Croatian service; he was widely renowned as the greatest Ottoman vanquisher of his time, and indeed, he only wrote this text while wintering on campaign.

2. "Even the great Homer naps."

3. "Perfect, because nothing is perfect under the sun, for even the strong does not give that sound, that is desired by the hand and mind."

the Hungarian language is impoverished: he who writes histories believes my words.

I have attributed to Zrínyi Miklós's hand the death of Sultan Suleiman: I learned this from Croatian and Italian chronicles, and Turkish sources also so record and attest to it. The reason that Istvánfi and Sambucus write it otherwise is because they did not examine the personal histories in the same way as they did the national histories.[4] However it happened, Emperor Suleiman fell there, that's for sure. I wrote about love too, but quietly; I cannot deny that it has troubled me, too; and then, love is not at odds with martial prowess, which I learned from this verse:

> *In galea Martis nidum fecere columbae,*
> *Apparet Marti quam sit amica Venus.*[5]

God be with us.

Count Zrínyi Miklós

4. I.e., biographies versus histories.

5. "The doves made their nest in Mars' helmet / So it becomes apparent that Mars loves Venus."

I DEDICATE THIS WORK

to the Hungarian nobles,
may God grant, that my blood
to its last drop, usefully
I may dedicate to him.

PART ONE

1 I, who once with youthful mind
Played with love's sweet verse,
Struggled with Viola's cruelties:
Now with Mars' greater poetry

2 Arms, and heroes I sing! The might of the Turks.
Him who was willing to undergo Suleiman's wrath—
That same Suleiman's mighty arm,
He at whose saber Europe trembled.

3 Muse! Not from rotting green laurels
Do you fashion your crown, nor from frail branches;
But from radiant, celestial, sacred stars
Is woven your crown, from moon and beautiful sun.

4 You, who virgin Mother art, and bore your Lord,
He who was eternal; and you who worship your Son
As your God and great king:
Holy queen, I beseech your mercy!

5 Give my pen power, let me write all as it was:
Of him, who for your son's sacred name valiantly died,
Forsaking this world, in which he had much good,
For which his soul lives on, though his body has died.

6 Allow his name, which still lives among us today,
To increase in fame, so that wherever sun rises
Pagan dogs would see: he who fears God
Can never die, but lives eternally.

7 The great Almighty looked upon the earth,
In one glance took in the world,
But most of all noticed that the Magyars[1]
Do not walk on that path which His Son ordered.

8 Saw He the Magyars' wandering,
Despising God to worship idols:
That they pursue their pleasure without restraint,
That they care only to stuff their throats,

9 That for His holy name there is no reverence,
For His innocent Son's blood, veneration,
No good deeds arise,
Nor for old men is there honor;

10 But much loose virtue and grave blasphemy,
Avarice, hatred, and false divination,
Unnatural perversion and slander,
Theft, murder, and eternal depravity.

11 Because of these, righteously grew His anger,
So he called Archangel Michael[2] unto Himself,
And in His great anger commanded him,
As before His holiness stood the archangel:

12 "Look, behold those stiff-necked and proud Scythians[3]
Who have far departed from being good Hungarians;
The good Christian faith they have trampled underfoot,
They glory in diverse religions.

1. The ethnic Hungarians.

2. The leader of the angelic armies; cf. Revelation 12:7.

3. The peoples of the Scythian steppes in Eurasia, who, according to legend, were the ancestors of the Magyars.

13 But see the world of the Christians,
You will find not among them any for whom I have done
greater good:
I brought them out of Scythia, which had grown too small
for them;
My Holy Spirit also came upon them.

14 From Scythia, I say, I brought them out,
As from Egypt, the Jewish peoples.
With my mighty arm I crush nations,
Everywhere I destroy, defeat their enemies.

15 In Pannonia,[4] flowing with milk and honey,
I established them in Hungary,
And I bless them in every circumstance,
I hear them, help them in every undertaking;

16 And even with noble hearts I blessed them,
So that one good Magyar could rout ten foreigners,
Nowhere at all have they found enemies so great,
That, like dust in the face of wind, they were not blown away.

17 My Holy Spirit I sent upon them,
To the Christian faith, by my Son, I brought them,
With sainted kings I gifted them,
Peace, dignity, I gave them.

18 But they, in return for so many blessings, ah, it is difficult
to say!
Ah, they are ungrateful, and dared to leave me;
They are not ashamed to betray their God,
To sink into every wretchedness opposed to me.

4. The Roman name for the Carpathian Basin, which encompasses both Hungary and Croatia.

19 Ah, I regret that so much good I did them.
Did I not raise up vipers upon my own breast?
But now, it is time to make it known to them:
I am the great God of revenge.

20 Go therefore, archangel: fly down into hell,
Choose one of those enraged Furies,
And send her into Sultan Suleiman,
To send him upon the Magyars in true rage.

21 I, then, will give the Turks such power,
So that they will thrash, destroy the wicked Magyars.
So long will the yoke break their stiff necks,
As until they acknowledge their abandoned God.

22 They will cry to me, and I will not hear them,
But I will laugh at their wretched plight;
I will not incline my ear to their complaints,
Upon their weeping I will not turn my eye.

23 So it will be until I have completed my revenge,
To the third and fourth generations there will be
punishment upon them,[5]
And if they do not in time come to their minds,
My eternal curse, my wrath will be upon them.

24 But if they return to me, repenting their sins,
From death to life I will again bring them.
Woe, Turk, is you, the scourge of my fury!
You are such, but I will break you, if these repent."

25 Archangel Michael began to intercede,
And for the true ones verily entreat,

5. Cf. Exodus 20:5.

"My God! Will you destroy the devout?
And for the sake of these impious punish them?"

26 But the living God is ready with reply:
"You wish to know my deliberations,
Or examine my great shrouded secrets?
Those which you cannot understand.

27 I will not spare the lash to fly upon my servants,
But he who needs not worry about his death,
I intend to fly to his aid,
And to revive his soul."

28 No further response did the archangel give God,
But spread his lithe wings to the sky,
Flew until—and did not rest—
Until Alecto[6] in hell he found.

29 With a hundred chains she is bound, a hundred restraints on her hands,
Her hair is snakes, and they writhe on her head,
Bloody venomous scum flows out her two eyes,
Odious sulphur fume spews from her disfigured maw.

30 This Fury the archangel unbound,
And with the power of God to her spoke thus:
"Alecto, God to me commands,
To send you into the Ottoman land.

31 Fly into the heart of Sultan Suleiman,
Raise up in his heart against the Magyars venemous fury,
To bring upon them his great and fearful arms,
To assail their lords and all their strength."

6. One of the Greek *Erinyes,* or Furies; a personification of the rage of the damned.

32 Glad is the Fury, delays not in hell,
Begins her flight into great Turkey,
At midnight arrives in Constantinople,
There alights in Suleiman's household.

33 And so, to better convince him,
And to not put fear in his heart:
Upon herself took the form of Selim;
Selim, the father of Suleiman (while he lived).

34 "My son, you sleep," so began her speech,
"And take no note of God's grace,
That He gave you strength, and courage,
Sound mind, sound council, and wealth sufficient.

35 You sleep now, and do not look ahead
At what a great storm Charles[7] is gathering before you,
And if you do not take note of it in time,
Here you will be crushed, in bed.

36 Believe, believe, on my august head,
If you give them time enough, they will do away with you,
Country and all, the infidels, faithless dogs;
For if there was unity, they would have strength.

37 There will be, too, because they treat; so charge them,
Do not delay, and give them no time to prepare.
Thus I made the Mamelukes[8] to flee,
Thus I defeated Campson,[9] and ruined the Syrians.

7. Holy Roman Emperor Charles V.

8. Also known as the Mamlukes, an Islamic dynasty that was based in Cairo, defeated by Selim in 1517, after which their land was incorporated into the Ottoman Empire.

9. Al-Ashraf Qansuh al-Ghawri, last Mameluke sultan of Egypt.

38 Get up, gird a sharp sword to your side,
Go with your armies upon the erring Magyars;
I will be beside you, and over all your affairs
I will faithfully watch, and over all your trifles.

39 Foolishness it is to fight against the Persians,[10]
Many good soldiers there to waste;
That our destiny will not falter,
God wants to teach us.

40 Ishmael to me great sufferings imparted,
But in the end, I still could not break him;
So on you many punishments Tamma[11] inflicted,
Vast portions of your forces with cunning he has defeated:

41 But against those Magyars we have always been victorious,
We do not even need to gather our forces very much,
Nor to spend as much, nor to lose as much,
Nor to doubt in our triumph.

42 Be not afraid that anyone should aid the Magyars,
Because I know well the idiotic infidels:
Until they see their own house on fire,
They do not help the houses of their neighbors.

43 Be not afraid, for lo! I have said I will be beside you;
The holy Mahomet also guides your hand.
And then also, dear son, the heroic man
Must cede some things to fortune."

10. Sulieman was at the time engaged in a religious war with the Shi'ite Safavid dynasty in Persia.

11. Shah Ishmael of Persia, enemy of Selim, and Shah Tamma, enemy of Suleiman.

44 So to Sultan Suleiman spoke Alecto,
And she, who had brought in her hand a venomous viper,
Released it into Suleiman's brain:
The snake does not rest until it has reached its destination.

45 From his shoulder to his chest, from his chest to his heart,
Wherever it slides, it leaves everything poisoned;
It enflames his heart and leaves it burning,
To writhe in pride and hatred.

46 Gleefully, Alecto disappears then,
For she saw how she enraged Suleiman.
He, however, jumped up: "To arms! To arms!" he shouts;
Alecto has driven him nearly mad.

47 Cries Suleiman, "O you, Courage,
Who goads me on to such great feats!
Greater are you than man, though in the guise of a man
I saw you speak and advise.

48 Suleiman is ready; he goes whence
You have commanded, he piles infidels in heaps;
I will bathe my steed in a lake of Christian blood,
Cities, fortresses I will cover in ashes."

49 Rising from bed, he commanded
That every officer should establish his camp,
Along with select men, each according to his ability,
Anyone who might bég or timar be.

50 And that in Drinaple, by the waning of May
The entire army would reside in camp.
The chausses[12] are sent in white turbans
To proclaim this to the armies in every nation.

12. Couriers.

51 Meanwhile Suleiman mounted his best horse,
And his generals he called out to council,
On a flat hill, not far from his gardens;
There he spoke to them thus:

52 "Generals and bashas, you wise soldiers,
By virtue of whose cunning I rule many nations!
You are the pillars of my power,
You, the victors over the pagan Christians.

53 Our current situation you can see:
It does not befit our kingdom to idle,
What we have won by sword, we cannot keep by council;
The empire craves arms and mighty soldiers.

54 Thus we won the Christian world,
That, which would rather pay tribute
Than honorably draw sword against us;
Thus do we honor Muslims.

55 Still, those who march against us, though not many,
Remain, and they dare to show their teeth:
Fools, they don't know that it is better to admit
Defeat than incur harm.

56 The Magyars are these, who have lost their head;
Like a broken ship, by the wind they are tossed.
Since I took the life of Louis,[13]
Many still vie for the crown.

57 True, I do not deny, that if there was unity
Among them, indeed, we would be given much cause for worry

13. Louis Jagellion (Louis II of Hungary and Bohemia), who was killed in the monumental Battle of Mohács in 1526, when the Ottomans firmly planted their rule over Hungary.

By the few Magyars, and they would harm us;
Our radiant crown they might smash.

58 But the scourge of God now alights upon them,
Greed, hatred rule over them;
There is no fraternity amongst them, nor wise council;
Therefore, their shining crown is falling.

59 We see with our own eyes the mercy of God,
For he has destined the Hungarian realm to us;
We can always face Tamma in the future,
Let us now ruin the Magyars and their realm.

60 I swear to you upon the living God,
Upon our magnificent crescent and my keen sword,
This night Mahomet in my father's guise
Told me these things with wise words.

61 Captain Arslan also writes me from Buda,
That I should not doubt in my victory.
Behold, I bring this letter also before you;
Read it aloud, scribe, let us consider it."

62 Now a Turkish scribe with loud voice reads:
"Invincible emperor, he your slave, Arslan,
Captain of Buda by your grace,
Humbly writes you with bowed head.

63 If you wish to know the affairs of the Christians,
They have allowed their situation to worsen;
Charles, from council to council
Has himself carried, pondering matters of religion.[14]

14. Charles V had involved himself deeply in the escalating conflict between Protestants and Catholics, and had begun promoting the Council of Trent as an authoritative political solution to religious disunity.

64 Nowhere does he have ready troops, and he does not even
think,
Like a madman, that he may sometime need them.
And Maximilian[15] lives among the Magyars
Tranquilly, only eating and drinking.

65 The Magyars, indeed, are the most idle of people;
Each hates the other, like dogs;
They have no generals, and even if they had, these
Never listen to the officials of state.

66 My lord, if ever you had the chance to do battle,
There are no others in worse a state;
It seems that even now, in Hungary
I see a river of blood, a multitude of infidels lying in heaps."

67 The generals, having heard Arslan's report,
And seeing above all the emperor's resolute will:
None dare to bar his way,
But each advises agreement to his purpose.

68 Not long after, from great Asia
A great many armies arrive, which were across the sea;
Many numberless Tatars[16] from the Meotic lake[17]
Who were dispatched from the Praecopian khan.[18]

69 Young Deliman[19] is the leader of these,
Son of the great khan and great ruler;

15. Holy Roman Emperor Maximilian II.

16. A Turkic ethnic group who had previously devastated Hungary in the thirteenth century.

17. The northeastern part of the Black Sea, which at one time had been a separate lake; the center of Tatar power.

18. The local *khan*, or ruler, of the Meotic Tatars.

19. Deliman will be the chief warrior fighting on the sultan's side.

Twenty-five thousand number these, and all expert archers,
The select from among many hundreds of thousands.

70 A light force, and brave, and fast like floodwater;
It appears as if every one in his hand carries death,
Because on the backs of good steeds, they hold faith only in good arms:
They carry no provisions, neither camp gear nor medicine.

71 They say: That Deliman, when many nations
He had wandered to see famed cities,
In Galata he saw beautiful Cumilla,[20]
Cumilla the beautiful, Suleiman's daughter.

72 Cumilla's fine hair entwined the heart
Of youthful Deliman, and all his desire;
One look stole all his strength
So that without her, he wishes not to live.

73 Then he went home, and now in fair battle returns,
Wondering how he could win the beautiful girl.
Unexpectedly, the wretch was disappointed,
Because by then Cumilla had been married to Rushtan bég.

74 Now with restless regret he stands, or sits;
The wretch's eyes unceasingly fill with bitter tears
From which his heart cools like freezing ice;
His mourning mires his life in death.

75 Guard yourself well, General Rushtan, against this one,
For like an enraged wolf, he seeks your death.
The powerful Deliman cannot bear his sorrow,
He will take, if possible, his revenge on you.

20. This romance, portrayed primarily in part 12, will play a significant role in the events of the seige.

76 After the Tatars, five massive hordes:
You would think, from afar, that they are screaming demons.
These too arrive in Drinaple,
Mighty Saracens, tried in many battles.

77 In each one there are six and six thousand men,
Each man dares take on three;
His horse like a falcon, he like a wraith,
Turning as easily as a bat of the night.

78 These marched on Crimson Head[21] with Suleiman,
These defeated King Louis with lances,
Warriors to the man, and not with breastplates
And shields are they armed, nor with thick mail.

79 Before these goes the champion Amirassen,
He is also black, and his horse too is Saracen.
His beloved steed is Karabul, whom he proudly
Struts at the head of the army.

80 They say that Karabul in great Arabia
Was conceived by the wind with a famous mare:
It is believable, too, for not in wind, nor in fire
Is there such excitement, such speed, as there is in him.

81 After Amirassen, three captains;
One of them Olindus, who by his wits
Became greater and greater an officer; finally became the
captain
Of a quarter of the Saracen army.

82 The Syrian king, wise Menetham
Sent the second: this was handsome Hamvivan,

21. Colloquial name for the Persians, who wore red-capped turbans.

From among the Saracens, to Syria he came;
But the third was cruel Demirham.[22]

83 Demirham the strong, he whom there was none stronger
than
Anywhere where Suleiman ruled:
For an oak tree he pulled out by the roots,
And beat to death a great elephant with his fists.

84 The fifth, Alderan,[23] elder brother of Demirham,
Was the quartermaster of the Saracen horde,
He, the interpreter of all dreams,
And explicator of Mahomet's writings.

85 After these come the powerful Mamelukes,
But they are wretched, because they have no leader.
To Suleiman they have recently become vassals;
In great and fertile Egypt they are residents.

86 Kayer bég comes with them, to whose shame
Mehmet Junnus basha was made a superior
By Emperor Suleiman; for he fears him,
And so to great honor he dared not elevate him.

87 These twenty thousand, good horseman were,
Because from Tommembey[24] they learned warfare;
And though they were composed of various nations,
Under wise leadership they were unified.

88 Not far the Cirkas, indeed a neighbor people
Of the Mamelukes, march in ordered ranks;

22. After Deliman, Demirham will be the other great warrior on the Ottoman side.

23. Aldaran will play a pivotal role in the final battle described in part 14.

24. Timur Lenk or Tamerlane (1336–1405), central Asian warlord who tried to restore Mongol supremacy; his descendents founded India's Mughal dynasty.

These may be fifty-two thousand strong,
For the Zinches, Getas, Barsts are with them.

89 They themselves elected a captain;
Him they call triumphant Aigas[25] basha,
And indeed they did not name him so in vain,
For he was the cause of many nations' ruin.

90 After Aigas basha come many Chagatays,
Tatars from deepest Scythia,
They believe in the Al-Koran, but by their green cambric
One can identify who are Turks, who are Tatars.

91 These, like ants, blanketed the earth,
Or like wheat, wide fields;
Everywhere gleam only arrows and scimitars,
And everywhere their identical dread flags fly.

92 These have never gone any place
That they have not conquered by arms,
But instead I say, they have destroyed
Everywhere that they have wandered on the earth.

93 Indeed, when these made war upon the Turks,
They all but entirely destroyed them;
But it is for our sins that they were left alive,
So that they could remain God's scourge.

94 Lo, the Scyth Tamberlane[26] defeated the Muslims,
Captured Bajazit, the great khan, alive.
Even then we could see the power of God;
He plays with men's destinies like toys.

25. After the Aegis, the shield of Zeus.
26. Also Tamerlane.

95 Never were the Scythians defeated by anyone,
Nor did danger ever threaten them;
King Mithriades[27] dared to disturb them,
But, tell you me, what could he accomplish?

96 They heard of the Romans' great power,
They never saw any power over themselves;
Great Alexander saw the bravery of the Scythians:
How difficult it is to occupy a sheer cliff.

97 In four camps these travel proudly,
In each are twenty thousand archers;
One of them is commanded by the black Saracen,
The other three: by Uldair, Lehel, and Turanchen.

98 Who could number the ocean's waves,
Or the Hercynian Forest's[28] countless leaves?
Only he could count Suleiman's peoples,
And record the massive armies.

99 For everyone heard: That Suleiman is going out with his armies
Upon the Christians, and that many Muslims are going:
Each hurries with his army after the emperor,
Each glories in the ruin of the infidels.

100 For beyond the beautiful Indus's waters live no Turks,
Nor to their emperor do they pay tribute:
Even so, comes here King Atapalik,
Because he wants to see how the Christian is destroyed.

27. Most likely King Mithradates II of Parthia, a proto-Persian ruler who fought wars in Scythia with limited success.

28. An ancient forest that stretched from the Rhine River in the west to the Carpathian Mountains in the east, infamous for its density and impassibility. The Black Forest is part of its remains.

101 Oh, whence will this great cloud spill?
What part of the world will it crush?
For the great wrath of God he will see,
Who this, falling upon himself, will see.

102 Like clouds do the sky, so covered the earth
Those many massive armies and foreign nations.
And we have not yet counted the Asian peoples,
Nor the European fighting forces.

PART TWO

1 Buda's overlord Arslan bég learned
That on his advice, peace shall be unraveled;
Thought he, delay is harmful in everything,
But most of all, idleness hurts in military matters.

2 His mind, too, was restless,
But without intelligence. Though he was unrestrainable,
In all his affairs he was exceedingly indeliberate,
And so all his affairs ended badly.

3 Without his lord's knowledge he gathered many forces,
With these he hoped to win favor,
If he should somehow defeat the infidels,
Or win some fortified castle from them.

4 Openly he declared: he will lay siege to Palota,
Before no one does he hide his intent,
But he boasted: he will tear down its tower,
And cut Sir[1] Turi György's neck.

5 Meanwhile he wrathfully gathered together his army—
Someone must have girded a scimitar to his waist—
The general did not cease to broaden his camp,
And before many days, added ten times a thousand swords.

6 He laid siege to Palota with so many troops under his
command,
With many cannons, and plenty of artillery;

1. Here and elsewhere in the poem, a Hungarian word has been translated as the English "Sir."

Wasting no time, by much cannon fire,
Moré's Bastion he began to brutally pulverize.

7 Turi is ashamed to be behind stone walls
Entrenched; he wants to be encamped.
Like a powerful lion, he does not delay in his cave,
When hunters find him asleep.

8 He bursts out with fury, he unsheathes his many strong
claws,
Mauls the hunter into pieces, strong nets he breaks,
Wherever he turns, he spills much red blood:
So Turi acts, besieged by the Turks.

9 Breaking ranks inside, with two hundred soldiers
He sallies forth from Palota, with famed knights all,
He struck upon the Turks with measured daring,
Many of them he cuts down with heroic prowess.

10 Guards he does not find, for indeed they sleep,
It is midnight, and they snore peacefully.
They fear not Turi, and do not even think,
That such a thing the Magyars might attempt.

11 Kurt aga was at the very edge of the camp, near the castle;
Out of stupid daring he pitched his tent there,
Around him three hundred janissaries slept,
Upon those Turi György bravely charged.

12 Very soon one hundred and fifty Turks are fallen,
Still Kurt aga barely wakes from his dream,
Because at dinner, he drained many cups,
And swore many oaths unto Turi's peril.

13 With naked sword he runs out from his tent,
Cries for help, which he expects from Arslan,

He calls out his fellows from under their tents,
But these all take greater concern for themselves.

14 Likewise now he wished to mount his horse,
So he could flee to Arslan's camp,
There Tót Balázs caught him and struck off his head,
And his rich tent the Magyars pillaged.

15 In their deep sleep many janissaries are killed,
But the leap is not long from dreams to death;
Wine spills from the full throats of many,
All of them, there, reap drunkenness's reward.

16 From the three hundred, fifteen escaped,
It is they who give General Arslan news of all this;
In his anger he all but split in two,
Quickly, with two thousand he hurried that way.

17 Turi has already returned to Palota,
So Arslan did not find him there,
But saw he the much Turkish blood spilled there,
Found corpses, many broken tents.

18 He retreats to his camp, swearing profusely,
Promising to the prophet Mahomet
That Turi he will skin lengthwise
For the occasion of Kurt aga's funeral.

19 The charming rosy dawn meanwhile arrived,
Gilded the world with dew and light,
With its rich beauty, brought joy to all;
Only you, Arslan, it depressed.

20 So with large cannons he quickly destroyed
Moré's Bastion, and leveled it to the ground,

He jumps on his steed, blew his horn,
To the bastion's siege he directed his men.

21 Every day he ate opium,
So that he could be crueler to Christian blood,
Even by morning from drugs he was drunk,
So that he knew not even his own actions.

22 He dashes toward the bastion, and curses its captain,
Night-bat and thief he decries him,
But answered him Turi György's artillery,
Which tore his horse in two beneath him.

23 If quickly the janissaries had not caught him,
The second cannon-blast would have shot him,
Thus humbled, he ran away from there.
Of drunkenness, such is always the reward.

24 The good general must live without wine,
Intoxicators he must not even have with him,
If he wishes not to make a black mark on his good
reputation,
And not to have his army suffer because of him.

25 For how does he differ from wild animals,
He who willingly divorces himself from reason?
He whose head is full of vapors from excessive wine
Cannot tell good from evil.

26 Arslan was drunk with wine and narcotics,
Received injury and shame from the sober captain;
He lost Kurt aga, and his own sickly self
He barely rescues from danger.

27 But on the siege he also lost two hundred men,
Because with steaming eyes he watched the ruined bastion,

Because within the bastion, two trenches protected
Palota, which the captain had just dug.

28 Two good horsemen he also lost in the battle,
Also his own younger brother, Durmis, on the second siege;
It is now the tenth day that he is sprawled on the mound,
All his actions lead only to unrightable harm.

29 But now Luftis aga terrified him,
Because he brought news of arriving Christian
reinforcements,
Arslan his tents quickly picked up,
With fear and trembling from there escaped.

30 This was the end of Palota's siege,
This was the end of General Arslan's wrath.
Turi kept his good reputation,
And there was peace for Palota.

31 On the tenth day of St. Iván's season[2]
Suleiman departed from Constantinople
With that tremendous army: waters draining,
Great mountains leveling, cities destroying.

32 A black Saracen horse was beneath him,
But one could not draw a finer one on canvas;
You would not think that his slim feet ever touch the earth,
So beautifully does he smoothly and silently trot.

33 His great bloody eyes bulge,
His sleek head is topped with a well-placed tuft,
Out his nostrils fiery breezes blow,
His mouth spews foam, as like an ocean god's.

2. St. Ivan's Day is the summer solstice, which would put the sultan's departure in late June or early July.

34 He bows his head under his high-arching neck,
The wind blows his short, shaggy mane,
With his wide chest, an elephant he resembles,
In claws, sleek sinews, a buck he surpasses.

35 Gracefully, quietly under the emperor he trod,
But should another have wanted to touch him—
Like a swift falcon, when alighting on wings,
Or like a fleet squirrel jumping from tree to tree.

36 On the saddle, dignified, the emperor sat,
A thin white cloth on his head,
Two sheaves of heron feathers line the width of his cap,
His beard is sheer white, his appearance is pale.

37 His fine golden tunic hangs from his shoulders,
His dolman is of the same material,
A mighty Misrian sword hangs down his side,
Which Sultan Musa won from the Greek emperor.

38 With terrible majesty he glances to either side,
One could easily tell that he carries weighty thoughts;
These carry in his heart flame and sword,
These are a great threat to the Christian world.

39 Those many cavalry, densely packed before and behind him,
Many lands have shrouded in terror;
You would think that a great forest rides before and after him.
Janissaries, like ants, cover the earth.

40 Many numberless cannon, which stone walls break and destroy,
Are hauled after, with the supply train;

Also many siege cannons, which spill Christian blood,
Ammunition, gunpowder, all manner of food.

41 All manner of carpenters' tools, great strong ropes,
Lumber and anchors, from which to make bridges.
Advisor Ali Portu commands these;
Cannons, wagons, and all tradesmen.

42 Many work horses come after these,
Long-necked camels and powerful mules,
Cattle, donkeys, and ox-carts;
Six elephants also, bearing many people.

43 Ahead of the sultan, two miles distant, go
Sixty-three hodjas[3] who scatter money on all sides
To all the poor, so that these from God
May incur favor for the sultan by their pleading.

44 I must write the truth, listen to me now:
Though Sultan Suleiman was our enemy,
Only his faith being pagan aside,
Perhaps never was there such a lord amongst the Turks.

45 Even aside from that, I can confidently say,
Amongst pagans there never was upon this earth
A man so honorable and wise, who in so many wars
Was victorious, and over many nations.

46 Honor and intelligence were equally present in him,
Prowess in battle was acute within him,
Had cruelty not made a mark upon his heart,
Maybe even amongst Christians he would have been the
greatest.

3. Turkish priests.

47 But when he had his son, Mustapha, killed,
Then he made himself most notorious for this,
In fact, he made himself hated by his nation;
For Roxa's[4] love he did this.

48 Fortune did not toy with him, as with others:
If she wanted to scare him with a blow,
Or with defeat in battle, or with other harm,
He was always prepared, with his intelligence;

49 He did not bend, like a twig, but like a boulder stood
Amidst the waves of the sea, steeled himself;[5]
So, if fortune gave him something good,
He became not proud, nor boastful.

50 Such a lord and such an army came upon our country,
And such a destructive cloud came down to our detriment,
Which not only for the Magyars' ruin
Would have been enough, but for the ruin of the world.

51 With a smaller force Alexander commanded the world,
So that all four parts brought him tribute;
Never did the Romans have such armies,
And even so they ruled the world.

52 Suleiman was diligent in his journey,
Soon from Drinapoli he came to Fejérvár,
And while still in Drinapoli he sent in advance
Petraf, so that he might assault Gyula on his way.

53 Petraf was the son of the Turkish sultan's aunt,
And he was the great beglerbég of Greece;

4. Another wife, who wished to be the mother of his heir.
5. Literally, "entered into himself."

The four thousand janissaries sent by the sultan
He commanded, and twenty-five thousand horsemen.

54 Thirty-two thousand Turks laid siege to Gyula:
Petraf fortified his camp,
With forty cannons he began to smash the tower,
And to level the beautiful white walls.

55 Kerecseni László was the captain there,
But the name of “captain” with great shame
He bore, surrendering the castle of Gyula in good faith,
Shaming himself and our nation.

56 But he reaped the rewards of bad men,
Saw the truth of Petraf’s oath:
Together with his soldiers he was taken into captivity,
From which they never found freedom.

57 Foolish is he who believes the Turk’s oath,
Especially if he entrusts his life to the Turks:
A Turk considers it a sin to hold to his word,
Especially if it is given to a Christian.

58 Look into the whole of Magyar history,
But even the ancient, Greek chronicle:
You will see, that the Turk cannot promise such
That he will willingly keep and obey.

59 Meanwhile the Turkish sultan hastened to arrive,
Does not know from which way to charge the Christians first,
Every which way wanders his wise and intelligent mind,
Which castle to invade: Eger, Sziget?

60 Then in Szigetvár, the famed Zrínyi
Was appointed captain by Maximilian;

He who was in Croatia and elsewhere bán,
It is he of whom my history shall speak.

61 The Turks' power he had tried not just once,
And in every battle, beaten them heroically.
In all Turkey he was well known,
Thus was he their greatest ruin.

62 For a Turkish camp's total defeat
It was enough to say: "Zrínyi is geared for battle!"
Like clouds before wind, it would scramble into motion,
And the Turks would run back to their home.

63 God gave him such power
That enemies before him, like sand, were swept away;
God knew well that he was a faithful servant,
And so blessed him in all his doings.

64 Zrínyi, one dawn, as was his custom
Whenever it was the break of dawn,
Before the holy crucifix would kneel,
And his pious mouth would begin to plead thus:

65 "Infinitely merciful holy God,
You who help me in all my affairs,
You are my invincible armament,
My shield, my barricade, my every hope.

66 Incline your ears from the lofty blue heavens,
In your mercy, hear my pleading,[6]
And judge me not according to my worth,
But by your inexhaustible mercy.[7]

6. Zrínyi is here paraphrasing Psalm 130, the *De Profundis,* which is part of the liturgy of the funeral mass.

7. Cf. Psalm 51:1.

67 Was I not formed by you of the earth?[8]
Did I not come from my mother's womb in grave sin?[9]
But by your grace was I cleansed of this,
And all my earthly goods I took from your hand.

68 You have given me nobility, with which I am content
And with a brave heart you have blessed me, and I have honor
Before all the world; but my worth cannot be worth
As much as all the good you have done to me.

69 Because my worth is as much to yours
As the water a swallow carries in its mouth
Is against the unfathomable ocean:
So is my worth against your mercy.

70 Even so, I am a wretched ingrate,
For to new sin every day I give much reason,
My Lord, wake me, I pray, when I sleep,
Wash me with your Holy Spirit, for I am foul and damned.

71 Remember not the sins of our fathers;
Indeed I pray, all sins forget:
For you, O Lord, not the dead but the living
Praise, and of your name speak great things.[10]

72 My Lord, you see also those pagan Turks,
How their mouths slaver, those faithless dogs,
Over how they should injure the Christians;
Their only purpose is to devise how they could wreak havoc.

8. Cf. Genesis 2:7.
9. Cf. Psalm 51:5.
10. Cf. Psalm 88:10.

73 Allow not, my Lord (though we deserve it),
That in your anger we be dashed to the ground,
That your holy name they would mock,
'Where are you, far from us?' they would boastfully say.

74 Show them that you are great, God,
That apart from you there is no God;
Who goes after you walks not in darkness,
But your path carries him to eternal rapture.

75 Not to us, not to us, O Lord, be glory,
But to your holy name give eternal praise.[11]
Save us, so that we may call on your name
For our help, and trust in you.

76 My Lord, I also implore your Highness:
You see, feebleness will soon be upon me,
Soon, there will not be enough strength in my body
So that I may crush your enemies, as before.

77 Receive my spirit, which longs for you,
As a besieged fortress for reinforcements;
Take it from my body, which is well locked,
Let it not sink under the sin-borne flood."

78 Thus did Zrínyi entreat God,
And so did God hear his plea.
He saw Zrínyi before the crucifix three times
Kneel, and answered this:

79 "Lo, I have heard your supplication,
Your fervent heart I have seen through,

11. Zrínyi is now quoting the *Non Nobis,* a medieval hymn drawn from Psalm 115.

I have taken your affair into my fatherly care,
Fear not, for I died not in vain for you.

80 Rejoice, my faithful servant, for you have invested well,
For upon your five talents, you have won five more,[12]
Upon the earth you have woven yourself a crown,
Which, gilded, you shall carry up to my Father.

81 There the angels readily await you,
In ordered ranks the cherubim stand,
They shall stand you upon my Father's right hand,
Together with you, they shall eternally rejoice.

82 I shall receive now your fine soul,
You wish it also, and you have recognized it well;
But so that an ever more glorious crown your head
Might ornament, behold, I give you this grace:

83 Martyrdom you shall suffer from the pagans,
Because for my name you shall bravely die.
Zrínyi, hear now what I will say,
Behold, your future I will recount:

84 Suleiman comes in force unto Hungary,
And before all he will assault your fortress;
He will pursue, like a sly fox, your death,
His power, his might, he will expend on Szigetvár.

85 But he will not see your ruin,
For at your heroic hands will he die,
Many thousand Turks must there perish,
And then will your spirit to me fly.

12. A reference to the parable of the talents; cf. Matthew 25:14–30 and Luke 19:12–27.

86 But your son, György,[13] will support your house,
He will garb your shining name in light,
Like a phoenix from the ashes, he will raise your nation:
With such wisdom he will uphold your reputation."

13. The author's grandfather.

PART THREE

1 Lord God, how fickle man's mind!
Man's wisdom crafts no immutable law;
That which he settles in his own thoughts,
Is turned by the will of God.

2 Suleiman turned his thoughts toward Eger,
To knock down its strong towers,
But God quickly deflected his intention,
For he soon turned his wrath on Sziget.

3 Here I will relate the cause of his anger:
Once he had commanded his armies
To hold their course toward Eger,
And to command the bridge over the Danube,

4 Bosnian chief-basha Mustapha meanwhile
Arrived with a fine army in the emperor's camp;
A famed warrior was he in Croatia,
Because by force he entered the castle Krupa.

5 The emperor recognized this man's worth,
Immediately gave him Arslan's command,
Also ordered him immediately to take the life
Of drunken Arslan, as he had taken note of his many faults.

6 It would have been better for you, Arslan, to lie low;
Without your master's word, not to do
Anything, let alone to foolishly initiate battle,
And with bad reports to fill your master's ear.

7 But Arslan did not dare await Mustapha,
Immediately left in Buda all his riches,
And tried to find the emperor's great camp,[1]
But even so he found his death.

8 The emperor gave to basha Mehmet Guylirgi
Bosnia, commanded him to hurry there:
That he should have the duty and responsibility
To render the Christians there harmless.

9 With two thousand horse Mehmet set forth;
Not many days later he arrived at Siklós,
There he encamped on the beautiful meadow,
There he pitched his own beautiful tent.

10 Skender bég of Siklós rushed to him,
Greets Mehmet, and said to him wisely:
"My lord, this to me is very shocking,
You do not know where you have encamped just now.

11 Or think you that you are in a peaceful land,
On good Turkish soil, free from enemies?
We are no longer on Drinapolitan soil,
But in the land of the infidel's outstretched sword.

12 Those Christian castles are not so far;
Know this, that in Szigetvár hungry wolves dwell,
Night and day, indeed, they walk this field,
Even in the countryside we cannot make our dwelling.

13 Of your arrival there has long been news:
Your dust makes your encampment obvious.

1. Ostensibly, to plead for mercy.

And if the shrewd captain of Szigetvár has heard,
On my head I swear, he has long been lying in wait.

14 My lord, because of him no Turk can stay:
No matter where his road goes,
Infantry or cavalry immediately find him,
Thus he loses his head, and leaves his body here.

15 Believe: even in the countryside we cannot stay,
From there also, by our feet we are towed away,
Even in the castle we cannot confidently rest,
So greatly does his fear intoxicate us.

16 For the sake of the holy Mahomet, I beg you, my lord,
Do not risk yourself here,
But instead follow my advice
And move your camp behind the castle wall.

17 The horses can stay out there in the countryside,
For the soldiers, however, there is room in the castle.
The loss will be less if the horses are lost,
Than if so many (and good) Turks go also.

18 Anyhow, my lord, you may seek danger for yourself,
But in doing so, you also pile wrath on my head;
Because of your actions, my name will suffer,
Therefore consider what you do, I beg, so that you do not
perish."

19 Mehmet, however, was unfamiliar with the Christians,
Because he had been raised in the royal court,
And he believed in the lunatic Al-koran,
That a Turk kills four Christians in battle.

20 So Skender he did not much believe;
Smiling to himself, he answered thus:

"I thank you for your advice, Skender Alboda,
But forgive me, it does not move my camp's location.

21 With a shameful reputation I would set out for Bosnia,
If here this night I would dare not stay,
And if before such nothingness I would so greatly tremble,
That I could not even find here a place for myself.

22 But these mellow clouds also reassure me,
For see, that they will presently array themselves in rain;
Even a small squad will find no quarter tonight,
Much less would there be passage for a large army.

23 But that which you speak of Zrínyi to me,
Even in great 'Stanbul[2] his news has come into my ear.
Lord God, if I would have such fortune,
That on this field I could make his acquaintance!

24 Because I have heard of his restlessness,
He has earned even the powerful emperor's fury;
He wanted to turn his scimitar on him,
But other circumstances stayed his wrath.

25 But he, too, will sometime fall on the dagger,
Like so many wandering foxes into traps.
This night, however, I will be unfortunate,
Because I will not see him, and I will rest without glory.

26 Skender, if you wish, let us two bed down together,
Beside warm coffee let us forge wise words,
Afterwards 'til dawn let us sleep in confidence;
Because I know with certainty, infidels we shall not see."

2. Istanbul.

27 Skender replies thus: "Confidently I stay here
'Til midnight, my lord; I will hold court with you,
And after that into the castle I will go,
And wish you a peaceful night."

28 Thus they two speak; meanwhile a retainer,
Unfurling on the ground a gilded leather cloth,
Placing two ornate velvet cushions beside the mat,
Perfuming the tent with Saracen incense.

29 There on the pillows the two sit down,
Between each other discuss many matters,
From small mugs they sip coffee,
Then afterward also eat dinner.

30 But after the meal a handsome Turkish boy
By his master's wish steps into the house,
A beautiful bejeweled tasha[3] sparkles in his hands,
A light cambric twists about his head.

31 From one of his shoulders his fine kaftan
He let down, began adjusting the kobza.[4]
He sat toward the window, crossing his legs,
Thus with the kobza's voice, he opened his lusty throat:

32 "Why should I complain, Fortune, against you?
If you increase every day my happiness,
You do not abandon me (as is said about you,
That in inconstancy is your every joy).

33 In spring you bless me with the gorgeous green forest,
The love-struck nightingale's singing,

3. A musical instrument.
4. A medieval instrument similar to a lute.

The airy birds' great variety,
Water's slow running, light breeze.

34 You do not envy me my beloved,
Rather, you help me to her, to make her love me;
Never do you steal my good humor,
Hourly you increase my pleasure.

35 In summer you give rest and graceful peace,
Alluring cypress shade, cool winds,
Fine needle-sewn splendid tent canopies,
Thirst-quenching, pleasant, perfumed waters.

36 In autumn with many fruits, citruses, oranges,
You bountifully gift me, with beautiful pomegranates;
You leave no game in the forest, because with those
You plentifully please me, and with good fowl.

37 But in winter, then when all are complaining,
Then my heart rather glories;
In the mighty tempest my heart does not worry,
For by a sublime, warm fire my body is warming.

38 And with my emperor I have great fame,
Amongst all I have great respect,
Never can my fortune be depleted,
I have a fine horse, sharp scimitar, beautiful lover.

39 But you are bound, Fortune, to my feet,
For by now you would have fled to my enemy
If you were free; but you bring no evil upon me,
Because you are bound, Fortune, to my feet."

40 So sang the child. But the great bán of Sziget,
Hearing of Mehmet's arrival by the dust,

Does not boast to the world; deep in other thoughts,
His good soldiers he calls at once together.

41 Eight hundred horsemen he picks, one thousand infantry;
With these, he thinks, he will carry out something great.
His good valiant horse he also mounted,
To his fair servants thus spoke:

42 "Soldiers, it is not necessary for me to tell you much,
Or for me to impart to you courage;
Each of you are such, that a national army
Could be under your command, and you could give heart
to others.

43 Remember all your heroism,
Your great, powerful deeds, your good renown;
Everyone act now with as much diligence,
As you have so far acted with valiance.

44 Yonder that pagan people sits fearlessly at Siklós,
Having left for Bosnia with twenty-six standards,[5]
They fear not Christians, speaking aloud
That, to our shame, they may on Siklós sleep.

45 Therefore my soldiers, let everyone obey,
Let no one by great daring be seized,
Await the word of all the captains and myself,
So that there might not be amongst us confusion.

46 And though Mehmet has an ignorant army,
And the basha's eye has never seen a bloody sword,
Still we believe this to be best,
For overconfidence would be our demise.

5. Indicating twenty-six platoons.

47 So then, my faithful servants, let us bravely set forth,
Three times shout the name of our Lord JESUS,
Hold back nothing from those pagan dogs,
For God is our leader, and our mighty guard."

48 Thus set out the Christian knights
Together with Count Zrínyi, resplendent flag-bearing battalions;
The clock had already struck two in the afternoon;
The flags wave, the arms gleam.

49 But to Siklós this night they cannot go;
At the break of dawn they are not far
From where the Turks in camp are sprawled;
But they ache to go, and even now saddle their horses.

50 A deep and long valley lies next to the camp,
The castle all but touches one end of it,
The other, however, toward Sziget
Lies, and comprises exactly one-quarter mile.

51 Sziget's captain with all his force
Ascended the valley in smart formation;
A sentry can be heard from the tower as he shouts dawn,
But the Christians are without sound.

52 On the other side of the valley a hundred horsemen stayed:
These, as soon as it had brightly dawned,
Trotting silently showed themselves,
Toward the Turkish camp held their path.

53 The Turkish forces took good notice,
But believed they, that these are soldiers from Pécs,
And that to the basha as an escort they arrive,
And therefore fear nothing from these.

54 But quickly from their hearts the doubt fell away,
As by the sword many Turks there were felled,
This small squad did not there long delay,
Retreating, they hurried back.

55 Screaming, shouting befalls the camp,
You would think demons are barking in hell;
Awoke the basha, did not hesitate in his tent,
Leaps onto his horse, in armed mail.

56 "Upon us, men" (thus he calls to the Turks),
"Are they who we have longingly awaited: with these dogs'
Blood we will paint our heroic hands,
Upon us is the time; be men.

57 For what have these thieving whores done to us,
They dared to come here, upon our flank,
Now their reward we will repay them:
Swiftly, then, on horseback pursue them."

58 These things having said, he himself exploded,
In his hand twirling a splendid plumed lance;
After him the flank, every man's horse runs as it may;
Only the basha's son did not greatly hurry.

59 Five horsemen kept at his side Rézmán,
This was his son's name, and he moved more slowly;
He was smarter too, though as a youth
He must now perish for another's folly.

60 As Mehmet was pursuing these to no avail,
Meanwhile Zrínyi from his hiding came out,
And to the basha's camp fearlessly went,
Because no one there could stand against him.

61 The soldiers all in one group he kept,
In the Turkish camp did not release them to pillage,
Carefully after the Turks he orderly marched them
Out from Siklós, from the camp he pressed them.

62 Rézmán noticed the Christians' flank,
And there began to curse his father's foolishness;
Toward Zrínyi he gallantly unfurled his flag,
To his father sent word of his grave situation.

63 Rézmán first Frank András from his horse
Struck off with his lance, then tore it from his throat.
His soul left his warm body first,
Even before he fell to the ground from his high saddle.

64 Csillag György stood by him with the flag,
To Rézmán's mighty lance he dealt a powerful blow,
The tough cornel-wood[6] lance he could not nick,
And could not parry its blow away from himself.

65 Mail there was on György's chest, but that could not hold it either,
Because strong Rézmán struck him through the heart;
Along with his pike, his life he snatched,
Flag and all, Csillag György fell dead.

66 Very soon Solymosi he beat down,
Thólnai Dömötör he killed with his sword;
Sir Sárkány György's head he took,
Young Jurcsics's life he took away.

67 Rézmán conducted himself thus with his scimitar,
But Farkasics Péter with his heavy broadsword

6. A type of dogwood.

Does no less than Rézmán,
For because of him dies aga Mehmet Butal.

68 Jussup oda-basha on the ground he laid out,
Kurt with one blow knocked to the ground;
You also died harmlessly beside him,
Jazichi Ahmet, for a grave wound finished you.

69 The horrendous blood-spilling I cannot record,
How the two spar, Farkasics, Rézmán bég;
Like living fire, wherever they tread,
Everywhere corpses are sprawled in heaps.

70 Everyone's foe is now before their eyes,
Turks and Christians are mixed together,
The groans of the dead, the screams of the living
Mingle with a great dust cloud in the heavens.

71 The Croat bán spied from the distance,
How the enraged Rézmán deals with his men,
His horse he goaded bravely with his spurs,
To where his men are all but in retreat.

72 Says thus: "Where do you run, you valiant people?
See who they are, who pursue you.
So this many Christians one Turkish child
Scares off-field?[7]

73 You want to escape into Siklós fortress?
You want to leave your lord here?
But he who will bravely follow me,
To him I will show victory."

7. This line deliberately truncated by the author.

74 Thus he spoke and no more; upon Rézmán he charged,
Who immediately in his hand held a powerful javelin.
When good Zrínyi closer approached,
With great vigor, daring, he hurled it at him.

75 Braced iron shield stayed the throw,
But that same iron shield it broke through,
But into the armor it could not pass;
Zrínyi with sharp broadsword struck Rézmán.

76 This the leaden mail could not stop,
From Rézmán's shoulder pours red blood,
Even through all this the valiant Turk does not retreat,
But with sword dares to strike Zrínyi.

77 Mehmet too meanwhile arrives from afar,
Sees the predicament of his son, Rézmán bég,
If help does not arrive soon,
Thus his only son's life will come to an end.

78 Like a boulder falling from a mountain,
Whose way cannot be blocked,
With great speed falling, standing trees wrecking,
Cleaving, smashing, wherever it rolls, stopped by nothing:

79 So Mehmet, seeing his son's peril,
Whoever he comes across, takes his life;
Kills, slashes, destroys, and rends, those who his path
Would stay, or his flight.

80 But when he arrives there, he sees his son dead;
Consider it, is there sorrow in his heart?
As when a wild tiger sees her cub die,
Both the hunter's net and herself she thrashes.

81 Thus says he to good Zrínyi: "Either you lay me out
Beside my son's body and remove my head,[8]
Or I will henceforth spill your blood,
And eagerly devour your stone heart."

82 Alongside such words to the great count, he struck,
Splitting his heavy helm in two,
And if the basha's sword had not turned,
That would have been Zrínyi's last hour.

83 God's angel stayed that blow,
In Mehmet's hand turned the scimitar,
Immediately Zrínyi returned a blow for the blow,
And along with his sword, his right hand he struck off.

84 Horse and all, to the hard ground Mehmet falls,
The knight Zrínyi jumps quickly after him:
"Mehmet, badly you avenge your son's loss,
Now you will follow your son's soul!

85 But fear not, for you die not without glory,
For behold, you were killed by the hand of Zrínyi."
So saying, he released his soul from his body,
For his head fell from his cruel breast.

86 At Mehmet basha's death were frightened
The entire army of Turkish soldiers,
Flag and all they were ready to run,
When they were stopped by Pécs's olay-bég.

87 To the Turks with a loud voice he called thus:
"That good soldier Mehmet basha was lost,
But we run? Is this to be the vengeance
For his noble blood, that his forces flee?

8. These two lines were rearranged slightly for ease of translation.

88 What part of the earth do you wish to live in,
What sort of people do you wish to go before,
If you will flee from the side of your dead lord,
And leave his body beside his son?

89 Ah, let the world never see such a thing,
That after such loss the Turk should show his back!
But even in your flight I see no purpose,
Except that with our blood we should paint the infidels' swords.

90 There is one hope for the defeated,
That he cannot hope in victory.
Is it not better to die as a man,
Than to live in shame before the eyes of all?

91 I, I—if your invincible hearts
Dare as much as your hands can accomplish—
I will be your victory-leading commander,
Or with eternal glory shall die."

92 So saying he took hold of his powerful strong lance,
And threw from his horse, dead, Marko Szila,
Then Tót Bence and an infantry vajda;
Also Cserei Pál's shoulder wounded.

93 Cserei Pál cannot keep himself on his horse,
Helplessly falls to the hard ground,
Ibrahim olay-bég already stands above him;
Then began pleading the wounded Cserei Pál:

94 "Noble man, hurt me not, for I am your good captive,
Plenty of silver, gold coin I can give for myself;
I am Zrínyi Miklós's main man,
I will not long wear your iron."

95 Heartlessly Ibrahim grins;
Says: "I do not glory in your monies,
Leave them at home for your sons and children;
My treasury shall not be poor without them, should I live.

96 You ask mercy from me, but Zrínyi has prevented it,
Because Rézmán's request he did not hear,
The noble basha he cut to the ground;
Therefore it is Zrínyi who kills you, sly fox."

97 Pál in his last hours greatly grieved,
To the merciless olay-bég thus called:
"Though this be my final hour,
Your life will be the price for mine.

98 You will not long boast of my death,
Not far awaits you merciless death;
By a strong arm your soul will fly to hell;
I, however, am eagerly awaited in heaven."

99 Laughs the merciless bég, then struck him
When Pál wanted to say more,
With his sharp scimitar sliced his larynx,
His life and his speech ended once and for all.

100 Alongside the blow thus he spoke:
"My future only the good God knows.
But die you now, and tell in heaven,
How Ibrahim olay-bég is going to hell."

101 From elsewhere Farkasics, like a roaring lion,
Pagan Turkish bodies piles in high heaps;
Slain by him lay Durlik aga; Rézmán
Basha's replacement also lies, eating the ground.

102 To him is given a wide and expansive path,
As everyone flees before him, wherever they can,
Not unlike when they fire the cannon,
And it carves a wide opening until it reaches its end.

103 Only you do not run, great giant Rahmat,
Unto Farkasics you bring your great bludgeon;
Long ago Rahmat left his horse,
Like a tower, he drags his club on foot.

104 In vain, Farkasics, you would await this with your sword,
You cannot harm him with your mighty broadsword;
And if you do not fell him with your gun,
Either by his sheer mass he will beat you down, or with his club.

105 So there he first grabbed his gun,
And the valiant Farkasics at Rahmat aimed;
Unfrightened was Rahmat, but bravely said:
"Cowardly dog, you wish to see me dead from afar.

106 Though you bring a cannon to bear for your protection,
You cannot hurt Rahmat with that;
Though you stand with fire against my mace,
You will still be food for dogs and crows."

107 Then Farkasics fired into his massive chest,
But the tall giant was not felled;
With his club he smashed Farkasics's head,
And beat him to the ground, half-dead, alongside his horse.

108 Rahmat, too, let himself fall on Farkasics,
For by his wound he could stand no longer;
Cursing, he released his soul,
Which had held his body so proudly in life.

109 There is no opposition left to Zrínyi's men,
Because the Turkish soldiers are running before him.
But here comes the vicious olay-bég on foot;
He does not run, but wants to die still.

110 Only half his helmet is on his head,
The rest all broke off in the many clashes,
His scimitar is broken, only half in his hand,
He is soaked in foul dust and Christian blood.

111 A hundred holes are in his shield, a hundred spear tips embedded,
Now the entire infantry has him surrounded,
But as the cliff is not hurt by the ocean's foams,
So the infantry are helpless against the bég.

112 But as soon as Zrínyi Miklós saw this,
To there on horseback he immediately rushed,
He did not allow the noble olay-bég to be hurt,
For he too admired his great prowess.

113 Thus calls Zrínyi: "Give up, sir, yourself,
Enough have you proven your honor,
For which sake I desire not your death.
I am Zrínyi; be not ashamed of your surrender."

114 Then his sword fragment the bég tossed aside,
For at Zrínyi's name his heart softened.
To the great count's knees he fell with such words:
"My lord, at your name, the bég has surrendered himself.

115 Know this, that to no one else I myself
Would have given; I would still raise my arm,
For an honorable olay-bég I call myself,
And in beautiful Pécs I keep my residence."

116 After this, the great bán his trumpet blew,
His own fine army called all together,
For the glorious sun had driven off its steeds,
And into the ocean-sea herded them.

117 The basha to his camp had himself carried,
Marched a dutiful sentry about himself,
There he slept that night. What happened the next day,
I entrust to the fourth part of my history.

PART FOUR

1 Man scrambles, fatigues, grasps at the world,
He expects it to yield constant happiness;
He does not believe that Fortune will snap apart
In his hands, and after a little sweetness will yield a hundred agonies.

2 He who is often given wide berth by misfortune,
Will sometimes see it crash down on him, with interest;
The higher capricious Fortune's mountain perch,
The greater the destruction and injury that she will visit on him.

3 Fortune delights in man's fall,
So she lifts him up, placing him even in the heavens,
That she may delight in his even-greater fall,
Like a mountaintop shepherd delights in a boulder's tumble.

4 A far-flung example I will not give you,
Though I could provide as many as I have hairs:
Mehmet basha's affair you have heard well,
He sat high with confidence, and lo, down fell.

5 Happy is he who is less conceited,
But with a ready heart awaits Fortune's whirling;
In all good, in all evil, her constant moving,
Fortune's many games we see.

6 Here, now, Zrínyi has good luck,
But even over him she has power,

Today he has a great victory over the Turks,
Tomorrow his noble head on a pike we will see.

7 You are happy, Zrínyi: you have beaten the Turks,
But perhaps before long you would pay any price
To have never seen the basha, Mehmet,
For he brings you only death and ruin.

8 But I am not allowed to say such things,
For his sainted spirit is with God, I know;
That he would die in Szigetvár, he knew, I know;
And so was not arrogant, I think.

9 For inconstant Fortune's gifts
He took in the same spirit as he would a red apple,
Which he could return at any time without sorrow
Knowing that one way or the other, it will rot.

10 But perhaps we have stepped out of our history,
And of Sziget's loss we have forgotten.
It seems to me, we may lighten this our burden
By speaking of him in whom we have great stake.

11 Fortune often toys with me, too,
Sweet and bitter alike she shows.
Though she toys with me, she cannot deceive me so
That I will not recognize her ever-changing nature.

12 Meanwhile, that beautiful sun with its beautiful dew
Gladdened the world with its ornate presence;
With dawn's pretty blush, it chased the night away
And lit the world's many varied spectacles.

13 Many loud trumpets then blared,
Many furious drums exultantly exploded;

All the good knights have mounted their steeds,
The infantry stand in ranks in their noble way.

14 Zrínyi has also mounted now, he stands before the host,
On his helmet a fine ostrich feather beats an angry wind;
His breast is covered in iron, giving him strength,
In his hand a great spear, and thus he speaks before the
host:

15 "That which we awaited from God, and which we asked
for by name,
Here, good soldiers, He has given;
Here on our enemies our feet tread,
Behold, God has mercy on us.

16 Let us take this from Him with much-grateful hearts,
Let us serve Him also with all our strength;
That which He has allowed us to do now with these,
Perhaps He will allow against greater foes.

17 Our dead companions also let us not leave here,
But according to their dignity let us give them burial.
For this will be to them our final remembrance:
By such good deeds we incur the blessings of God."

18 There Cserei Pál's body they mounted on horseback,
Then took the rest up off the ground.
Twice twenty were the dead heroes' bodies,
The Christian soldiers took these up.

19 Noble Farkasics they placed on a stretcher,
For he had not died by the horrendous blow,
But only barely lived, for in his head-bones
Perhaps there was not even one still intact.

20 Between the troops, all these are carried,
Friends and relatives gathered around them,
They encourage the wounded with good, noble words,
They bind their wounds, pity and mourn them.

21 But before all these go two hundred horsemen,
All armed, and all feathered Gleams each one's mail,
helmet, and sword blade,
On each one's back is a raging wolf-skin cape.

22 Not one of these had their lance in battle,
For instead they all carried carbines on their sides
Now lances they hold in their hands, and on each lance's end
A Turkish head sits impaled.

23 Two hundred infantry then follow these;
Each his own captive next to him leads,
Each has a cape, and a stalwart glance,
You would think, their feet do not even touch the ground.

24 Six Turkish agas' heads six horseman
Carry on great pikes, footmen stepping after,
After these they carry Rézmán's arms,
The basha-replacement's, and Mehmet basha's.

25 Three ostrich skin–clad lieutenants go after this,
Those three carry heads on high spears.
Now comes the olay-bég of Pécs after these;
You see, that he still sits on horseback, furious.

26 Afterwards thirteen Turkish flags are waving,
These, thirteen men on foot are carrying,
Afterward the flank comes in ordered ranks;
The flags wave; they are in high spirits.

27 Twenty large-necked camels come after the army,
The basha's tent they carry on their backs.
There are forty mules also, and cattle twice sixty;
These were all spoils on the plain of Siklós.

28 When close to Szigetvár they arrived,
Then the ordered ranks all stop,
Together giving thanks to the living God;
Three times his holy name they loudly shout.

29 Zrínyi from his horse there dismounted,
With his chief lieutenants strode into the church,
There rendered to the great God many praises,
Because this victory he ascribed to God.

30 Before the Holy Church infantry carbines crackle,
On the bastion monstrous cannons roar,
Smoke, shouting into the sky together spiral;
Perhaps even in the heavens the angels hear it.

31 Before the Holy Church onto an ornate carpet
The noble corpses are orderly placed;
Zrínyi saw them, upon his exit,
Thus he called to them with saddened heart:

32 "With what blessing shall I praise you,
O noble corpses, killed in Christian fashion?
For our precious homeland your lives expired,
We were honored by your noble blood.

33 Truthfully I say, I would that I could lie among you,
So that I would not envy your fortune,
For you sit now at God's right hand;
God be with you, then, for all eternity.

34 Perhaps that God with whom you now rejoice
A longer path has destined for me, and trials;
I have faith, that not long this tired-of body
I will leave here, and we will see each other in heaven."

35 Thus good Zrínyi from his dead servants takes leave,
Together with his lieutenants steps into the fortress;
There his son they have brought before him,
To whom his father such fair words spoke:

36 "Learn from me, my son, the fear of God,
Learn endurance and hardened courage;
Because you too must follow me;
Walk far and tire much, sweat."

37 Meanwhile great tables are set,
With Count Zrínyi the knights there sit,
The honorable olay-bég they also invite.[1]

38 Zrínyi hosts the knights all with glad heart,
Some he greets with fine wine in golden cup,
Praising how he conducted himself in battle;
Some he nurses with presents of words.

39 But as soon as good wine warmed their minds,
Each one, having put aside their sense,
Some with loud throats begin Croatian battle songs,
Some with weapons strutted battle dances.

40 One praises his horse, one his strong weapon,
One his companion, one himself, one the spoils,
Everyone, however, their lord's nobility;
With loud voices they cry and acclaim him.

1. This quatrain deliberately truncated by the author.

41 Just the olay-bég with sad heart sits alone,
With mournful thoughts his head is graying;
Amidst many warriors' voices only his heart cools,
Sometimes he is all but lost in great sorrow.

42 Zrínyi, seeing such great sadness,
Addressed the honorable Ibrahim with such words:
"Soften your sorrow, warrior, do not grieve,
Now with us you eat, drink.

43 That God which has given you now to captivity,
Has reserved for himself your way to freedom;
There is no cause for your sadness,
That fortune has now so dealt with you.

44 You did all that was in your power,
You cannot change God's will to something else.
Not as a captive do I hold you,
But as a noble guest, arrived by his own volition."

45 Replies the bég to Zrínyi, bravely into his eyes staring:
"O great-famed, but even nobler knight,
Who looks upon the defeated with mercy,
I rejoice, that here has brought me Fortune's wind.

46 Why would I be ashamed of captivity at your hands,
If you cause the Turkish empire to tremble?
If you debase our shining moon?[2]
Am I like the most of them?

47 Neither with my valiance do I ever boast,
For only God alone is valiant.
Only humbly your Highness I beseech,
That to such a captive you do a great mercy.

2. Reference to the crescent moon on the Ottoman flag and insignia.

48 Six weights[3] of silver I give for my ransom,
Horses fit for a lord, six I bring;
Take them from me with good faith, what with good heart
I give,
For thus I estimate my worth."

49 "I do not need your money" (thus replied Zrínyi bán),
"For gold, silver, I have enough,
But amongst the Turks one noble vassal I have,
His freedom my heart craves.

50 That vassal they call Radován vajda,
Aside from his honor, he has nothing,
Believe me, I have heard, that for his ransom,
The amount is less than that which you offer.

51 This one free, then I will make you free."
Here the bég kissed Zrínyi's hand,
Because the lord gave in to his worthy request,
For him, many prisoners would be bailed.

52 Meanwhile that mercurial news alit on its wings,
Faster than wind and bird it flew;
News, of which there is none more evil, nor faster to spread,
Which only gained strength in flight:

53 Wherever it goes, the basha's loss
With a thousand trumpets it announces, and his defeat;
It did not rest until it filled the emperor's ear,
That of the great emperor, that of Sultan Suleiman.

54 But after its fashion, falsely it proclaimed,
That Turkish forts the Turks have all lost,

3. About one hundred kilograms each.

And that Guylirgi basha was beaten by Zrínyi,
That not one escaped from battle, all he killed.

55 Verily, the emperor stumbled from such awful news,
Hearing these, he forgot himself;
But he acts as if he were unafraid,
And before the bashas shows a brave heart.

56 He does not believe the basha's severe loss,
Considering Mehmet's unspeakable intelligence,
But soon he cast all doubt from his heart,
Because the wounded[4] Islan brought sure proof.

57 From the battle he just barely fled Siklós,
He also brought brave evidence:
For a sharp spear-end was left in his back,
And on his head two wounds. Islan spoke to the emperor thus:

58 "My lord, who has the ocean-sea's waters
As the border to your name, and the skies;
I would wish, that I could come to you with better news,
Rather than that which I must bring by obligation.

59 Tayeleri Mehmet,[5] your courageous basha,
Desiring to undergo an untimely test,
At Siklós set up his camp;
And lost that, his noble son, and himself.

60 Zrínyi's sword devoured all this,
I do not believe many of us could have escaped,
But he sowed such fear even in the border forts,
That those about him are all but abandoned.

4. Perhaps "swift."
5. An alternate spelling of Mehmet Guylirgi.

61 I myself only barely and fleetly ran,
Truthfully, the basha and his son dead I saw,
Pécs's olay-bég in infidels' hands I left,
Everything was devoured by that infidel sword, my lord."

62 The emperor immediately called together his generals,
Once he truly understood these reports;
Says to them: "While we see enemies elsewhere,
Meanwhile that Croat bán, look how he ruins us.

63 All of us indeed would be worthy to be made fools of,
If we this Zrínyi would tolerate.
Now in our hands is our disciplining rod,
Let us leave peace for harmless Egervár.

64 Oh, what great punishment I will inflict upon you!
How you will pay with your blood!
You before all, audacious Croat Zrínyi,
With your head you will pay for Tayeleri.

65 Therefore, my bashas, immediately those forces
Call back, they who the rapid Danube
By my command crossed;
Immediately let them turn their flags back to me."

66 To Sokolovich Mehmet[6] he commanded,
(This his highest and favorite general was),
To give Kadilesker a thousand sheep,
That he would in the name of God scatter them to the
vultures.

6. Sokolovich Mehmet (1506–1579), who plays an important role in the epic, was a major Ottoman political figure, especially after Sultan Suleiman's death, when he became advisor to the next two sultans and the power behind the throne.

67 Herded a thousand sheep across the wilderness plains
Kadilesker, and left not one in its skin;
He was in the sultan's great favor,
Because he was the high priest and archbishop of their faith.

68 Many vultures landed on the ground, and blanketed the livestock,
With their monstrous hooked noses, began to tear.
Countless many crows crow everywhere,
Robber kites, thief hawks mingle.

69 But a miracle I tell you here:
Now comes a great eagle with angry claws,
Resembles a devil in its pitch-blackness,
An ox with its size and hideousness.

70 Three times it circled with its wings those sheep,
Moving its wings like galley oars;
Finally downward it turned its swift flight,
Chased, drove away all those birds.

71 Once there was not even one, then he landed,
Amongst those many carcasses he mercilessly strode;
But he did not partake from even one,
But in a dark cloud disappeared.

72 Kadilesker at this was verily afraid,
He knows that this future cannot be good.
Thus he addressed Sokolovich Mehmet:
"Incline, my lord, incline your ear to my word.

73 Though to you I need not speak much
Because this omen you fully understand, I know.
Our going unto Sziget I do not advise,
God forbids it by the birds, you see.

74 You saw how the condor chased the small ones,
But he did not even bother the skinned lambs.
Truly, this intones the emperor's anger upon
Us, because he cannot take Szigetvár.

75 He will chase us by all his strength, for his siege,
We will fly before him, like crows before the eagle;
I cannot speak well of the emperor himself, either,
For we lost the eagle's flight in the mist.

76 When we chanted toward Egervár a divination,
It showed that which we wished ourselves:
In Egervár will sit our emperor,
We, too, all will meet with fortune."

77 But neither did great Suleiman tremble from all these,
He shows a brave face in Mehmet's tent;
I do not know if his heart is as his mouth says,
But at bad omens he derisively laughs.

78 "Let us act such" (he says to Mehmet),
"As we know best, and as true men,
The rest we leave to the will of God,
Hungry birds do not scare us.

79 But a better omen for us there could not be:
Do you know, my good servent Sokolovich Mehmet,
Why those many birds the carcasses did not eat?
Because from Christian bodies they await better food.

80 Tomorrow, if God gives us health,
Let everyone's horses be ready and saddled,
Let God's beloved camp depart,
Mahomet takes great care for us."

81 The sun set quietly in the meanwhile,
And soon it was midnight-time,
Such a great accident befell the camp:
Two agitated horses broke out of a tent.

82 They run out of the tent with great violence,
The tent ropes they tear with their kicking,
They are destroying everything now with their heavy iron feet,
They run along the entire camp with speed.

83 The sleeping heads of some they crush, the stomachs of some,
They charge upon them, on some they collapse tents;
Some yell, some weapons seize, and rouse their friends,
Everyone suspects the infidels' treachery.

84 I know not from which one some words escape:
"If now bán Zrínyi Miklós were present here,
By my faith, all of us he would confound;
God forbid, that Zrínyi be here!"

85 Iskender Talisman[7] heard Zrínyi's name,
Did not hear the rest of his neighbor's speech,
He believes for certain Zrínyi's presence,
He runs, hiding everywhere, he cannot still his heart.

86 Cries the Turkish monk, "Zrínyi is upon us,
I saw him with my own eyes; let everyone flee!"
Flees, whoever hears this, few are those who remain,
Those who bravely stay with their scimitars.

87 Swelled the camp, from everywhere they run,
Some wage great war between themselves;

7. A priestly title.

Amongst alien nations, should they mix,
Everyone thinks his companion an infidel.

88 Whoever "infidel" shouts, there his head is taken,
For truly an infidel they judge him,
With horrendous cries the camp fills,
Men, horses, tents they confuse amongst themselves.

89 Already Murtazan basha has left the camp,
To look, to see, by what reason this happened:
With him, thirty hundred, all with horses,
Sent by Sokolovich basha.

90 But already Aigas basha, captain of the guard,
Because his shift was upon him, was circling the camp;
Numbered thirteen hundred his good horsemen,
When in the darkness he saw Murtazan.

91 He believes that this is the infidels' group,
With few brave words does he encourage his men,
Upon the Turks he launches his own troop,
He does not ask, does not even speak, just furiously cuts them.

92 By a great heavy lance many he beats to the ground,
For to him they are all strangers;
But no one can stand against Aigas,
He himself is strong too, and has a powerful troop.

93 Retreats Murtazan with all his people,
Flees his great army with great shame,
Aigas reaches Murtazan along with all his people;
He sees, he believes this to be the captain of the infidels.

94 With his mace he hit Murtazan heavily,
Which knocked him to the ground, against his will,

But he did not hurt him, so that he could gain information,
Bound, before a fire he had him hurriedly taken.

95 Such tumult hearing, the emperor Suleiman,
With countless cavalry walks amongst the camp,
Around him are many good janissaries with carbines;
He searches, from where there could have arisen such cacophony.

96 He is not afraid of Zrínyi, because he knows without doubt,
Even a bird could not come so quickly, on wings;
So everyone he fortifies, who, fleeing, he meets;
Finally quiet, by a small fire he stops.

97 Well, here Aigas basha brings Murtazan,
He wants to see by the fire who it is;
By luck he chanced upon the emperor,
Recognizing from afar the emperor, he called to him:

98 "Behold, great emperor, Zrínyi I bring you,
You can thank one of my club-swings for this."
But Murtazan shouts, "Well, do not hurt me,
I am also a Turk; I know you."

99 Aigas looks bravely into Murtazan's eyes;
Says: "Truly you do not deserve the Turkish name."
With such words he loosed his bound hands;
Murtazan does not dare raise his eyes.

100 There Aigas recounts to the emperor how he fared:
How Murtazan fled, and how he tied him,
From amongst the Turks too, many he beat,
Because they did not know the signal and did not recognize him.

101 Victorious Aigas in great respect stayed,
But Murtazan, because he shamefully ran,
Before the warriors was held in shame;
The emperor returned to the quieted camp.

102 Of the Turks three thousand lost their lives,
Because Aigas cut down a thousand of Murtazan's;
Some in their own running broke their heads,
For some, guns tore their chests, heads.

103 Much work had the powerful bashas,
And even the wise, great emperor himself,
To quiet the aroused people,
Indeed with difficulty, late were they made tranquil.

PART FIVE

1 From one direction, Suleiman, in great preparation;
From another the Croat bán, caring for the fortress;
Already his ear has filled with news of the emperor,
That he has set out for his ruin, with all his powers.

2 Zrínyi stands unshakably, mired in deep thought;
As great towering stone cliffs in high Késmárk[1]
Against which the winds struggle in vain,
Their powers expending uselessly on the siege:

3 So no anxiety shakes Zrínyi, nor any trembling,
Should even Atlas break down, or the great sky fall;
Because fear falls not upon the unmovable,
He who with a true cause and a good heart is armed.

4 Generals, vajdas he called forth,
The warring ranks he stood up front;
When all together he saw them,
With such words his wise mouth he opened:

5 "Fortune prepares no accidents for us,
She does not thrust upon us unexpectedly that which she
has built,
That which we with brave hearts have awaited, knights,
is here,
Battle, arms, before us, the preparations of the pagans.

1. A town in modern-day Slovakia, high up in the Carpathian Mountains.

6 Powerful Turkish emperor Sultan Suleiman
Brings upon us his wrath, like an angry lion,
To destroy and ruin us he desires,
His hope is in his many countless armies.

7 His every hope is in his forces' number,
His power, his strength are in his countless janissaries;
He rouses against us his many horsemen,
From many parts of the world gathered, pagans.

8 Foolish is he who places in these his trust,
Counting as an afterthought God's mercy;
God dashes his hopes angrily,
His cavalry, his infantry, and his terrifying weaponry.

9 For this He destroyed Pharaoh mightily,
Goliath He shamed by one child,
And the Philistines by terror;
With a vengeful heart He ruined pagans.

10 But mercy He gave also to those with humble heart,
All those that had their hope in Him,
Thus He gave mercy to the Jewish peoples,
To many holy kings and to the child David.[2]

11 Indeed, God's arm has not shortened,
His merciful ears have not been plugged;
How many times the mercy of God on ourselves
Have we seen, and tasted His many gifts.

12 With that enemy we will fight,
Who many times before us, like livestock, we have driven,

2. King David of Israel, whom God elevated to the position while he was still in his youth, and who wrote many of the Psalms Zrínyi quoted earlier.

Weapons, honor we have taken,
By the grace of God, we have often defeated.

13 We cannot believe, powerful warriors,
That our hands, though ready and firm,
Have with such grim trials finished,
For which we are honored by men.

14 It was a greater power, the great God,
Who for us fought with might,
To our hands, strength; to our hearts, courage
He gave, and from the pagans took these away.

15 Indeed, what He did for us at Siklós:
The merciful God, with countless Tatars;
Like a swollen river, they came upon us in number,
Easy prey they considered us.

16 God broke their ranks,
He dulled their hearts and their weapons,
Therefore they did not want to face us,
And we cut down from among them twice two thousand.

17 Without blood or exertion we defeated Ulman,
Who with great anger brought upon his great army.
But Ulman left behind countless prey,
There he left many agas, and Gyafer, his son.

18 Babocsa even now from the Turk Rinya's blood
Is warm, and the field is white with corpses;
The Turks of Buda also ran, like dust from the wind,
Before us, because God guided our weapons.

19 How strong a shield sustained me,
When from Babocsa[3] they blew away my steed
With a cannon, and for the second time the feather from
my helmet
They shredded; close I beheld my death.

20 Indeed, not long ago did we not see a miracle,
When God into our hands gave Korotna?[4]
We did not expect the walls' destruction by cannon fire;
Unharmed, we took its strong stone walls.

21 Arslan Yahiogli ran away before us,
He did not dare await our army-crushing weapons,
For he knew that the great God is with us,
And therefore we cleaved and killed them, 'til boredom.

22 On the field of Siklós Tayeleri Mehmet
Lost there his camp, his son, and his life;
Barely was there perhaps even one who could carry
the news
To the Turkish emperor, for all the others were lost.

23 Sooner would expire my life, O stalwart knights,
Than I could fully recount the mercies of God.
Nor does His all-powerful hand leave you now;
You, too, labor for His holy name.

24 From all sides Christendom looks to us,
In our capable hands rests all hope,
Never before has come gross shame upon us,
So are saturated with our fame the earth, sea, and sky.

3. Zrínyi waged a successful campaign in Bobosca, in Somogy County, in 1556.

4. Zrínyi fought another successful campaign to recapture Korotna, in Croatia, from the Ottomans in 1566.

25 Now must we redouble our fame,
Or with honor end our lives;
Time will not destroy our deeds,
As long as earth exists, and man sees sky.

26 It is also to our great honor,
That our enemy is Sultan Suleiman himself,
Who if we defeat, as we hope,
We will have defeated the world-judging emperor in battle.

27 To fight, however, not just for any reason
We must, but for our beloved Christian homeland,
For our Lord, wives, children,
Our own honor and lives.

28 May the pagan dogs see our bodies dead
Rather than that we should lose our many treasures,
Rather than that they should carry us on leashes,
Killing our fame along with our freedom.

29 To this goal will they turn all their skill:
To trick us, like fools, with oaths.
Foolish is he who gives Turks' words his trust,
For with his castle, he loses his life.

30 For Sir Amadi strong Visegrád
Gave up to the Turks, out of great thirst,
He paid with his life, and so regretted the affair;
Thus Sir Losonci also gave up Tömösvár.

31 Gave up Losonci, with great reluctance
Tömösvár's fortifications, with a simpleton's heart,
But quickly he paid, with his precious life,
And all his soldiers' loss.

32 We have nothing to believe the Turkish emperor,
Because he is not a man of his word;
He did not give Buda to the king's son,[5]
But with great treachery, kept it for himself.

33 But how would he give faith, he who has no faith?
How would we believe the Turks, who lie in all things?
We must die here, in this place,
Or we must prevail, trusting God.

34 Let this place and this fortress be our glory,
Or vultures' bellies be our tombs.
Either way, let us be men, and soldiers,
For thus live forever our good names.

35 As long as my head is upright, I shall be with you all,
I swear, soldiers, to God!
I want you all to act thus also,
Sharp swords in hand, swear."

36 With noble Zrínyi's words they were emboldened,
All of Szigetvár's men-at-arms
Before him in ordered ranks stood,
Their naked arms in their hands held.

37 As when that great wind from Késmárk breaks forth,
And is caught in that dense pine forest
Causing a great noise, it does not tire or languish,
Bends before it the soft, and the hard branch breaks:

38 Such a great noise comes from amongst them,
Because angry blood boils in everyone,
Each one craves: into enemies' blood
Soon to dip their hands, and into their hearts.

5. János Zsigmond, son of János Zapolya; see introduction.

39 There Farkasics Péter (for he had healed
Of that blow, which Rahmat had landed)[6]
Draws his scimitar from its sheath before the count,
And looking into the skies swears thus:

40 "Hear, you true God, my speech,
And you, noble count, my oath!
If from my country I withhold my life,
If I do not happily spill, where I must, my blood:

41 If, while I still live, I abandon my lord,
Or I devise here traitorous schemes,
God, with your vengeful lightning myself
Strike, and cast my soul down into hell."

42 Farkasics was Zrínyi's chief lieutenant,
His army numbered two hundred thirty-two,
Everyone had mail, sword-iron, and helmet;
Each one with loud voice thus swore with him.

43 As soon as the noble captain stood to the side,
Came with one hundred fifty swords Novákovics Iván,
A fierce tiger's skin is on his back,
And a terrifying eagle feather is pinned to his shield.

44 Novák is of Debelják's people,
And in his deeds is comparable,
Broke under his foot many a Turkish flag,
Prone under him were many Turks, many dead horses.

45 A hundred naked scimitars Dandó brings after him,
He himself is before them, strutting like a lion,

6. A confusion of identity on the author's part; actually, a different Farkasics Péter altogether.

He too thus swears, then stands aside,
After him arrives with a hundred Orsics István.

46 A mother could not have borne one braver than this,
One with stronger a body, nor larger,
You would think that Mars is walking, when you see him,
Many times, with only his eyes he chased away Turks.

47 Comes Szecsődi Máté, a great spotted goat-hide
Draped over him, and with armored weapons,
A great naked broadsword he holds with his strong hand;
Swears he, too, with a hundred strong men.

48 Well, Alapi Gáspár with four times fifty scimitars
Comes, covered in a panther's back,
In noble fashion, with ornate fine crane feathers,
He swells with prowess and intelligence.

49 You come, too, merciless Radován Andrián,
Because your lord ransomed you on the olay-bég's bail.
Believe, that the lion is no wilder than he,
When amongst the Turkish troops he is mingled.

50 He has sent already six hundred Turks to hell,
But he will send still a thousand: such is his purpose;
A hundred wounds cover his body, which he won in battles,
Most of them not long ago, when he fell into captivity.

51 Here Stipán Golemi with terrifying figure
Steps, like a mountain, with terror;
But he can never be hurt with weaponry,
Because tougher is his hide than iron and hard stone.

52 Behold, Bata Péter also with stately dress
Comes along with fierce Patatics Péter,

Papratovics Farkas comes with lithe body;
They were each with a hundred good men.

53 Kobács Miklós leads two hundred men alone,
For his friend Lieutenant Cserei Pál was lost;
Indeed, even a thousand he could worthily lead,
Because there cannot be in battle one more cunning than he.

54 Comes the scribe Balázs also with great Győri Mátyás,
Medvei Benedek with powerful Bika,[7]
I say, indeed with powerful Bika András,
Who Turk and horse kills with one blow.

55 Geréci Berta also fifty men leads,
Because the rest were lost at the olay-bég's hand;
Geréci himself was wounded on the head
In the last battle, in which the basha fell.

56 Juranics Lőrinc was a flag-bearer,
But not long ago came his vajda's death,
Therefore, for his worth they made him recently a vajda,
Because much courage in battles he showed.

57 Young Juranics, than whom a more beautiful youth
The sun's eyes could never glimpse on the earth,
Leads after himself twice fifty swords;
Orostoni Péter after him another hundred

58 Brings Horvát Radivoj a hundred men after this,
This with a hundred follows Bajoni Iván;
Guszics András with a hundred is in his footsteps;
He held Fort Zrin[8] against the Turks bravely.

7. A pun; *medve* means "bear," while *bika* means "bull."
8. House Zrínyi's ancestral castle.

59 Here now Deli Vid,[9] also, the scourge of the Turks
(Because he instructs them often in running);
He himself comes last, this powerful champion,
With him comes five times fifty fierce scimitars.[10]

60 It is not enough to compare this one to a lion,
Because he resembles the powerful army-destroying
    wrathful Mars;
It can be seen in his eyes, too, that death and fire he brings,
He carries a four-fathom[11] iron lance in his hand.

61 In a velvet mail shirt he dresses his frame,
A great marten-skin cap is on his head,
On that a hawk's wing shows its beauty,
A great, heavy shield weights his arm.

62 A large spur on his foot plows the hard earth,
A hard Fringian sword[12] supports his flank;
This was the flower of Sziget's knights,
Wise, strong, fast, fierce, when he wants.

63 These all swear to Sziget's count,
That with him in the fortress they want to die,
And that from beside him 'til death they shall not stand
    apart,
But will be faithful to him and the country.

64 Completing the muster, dutiful Zrínyi
Began to inspect the state of the fortress,
Raising cannons onto bastions, in order,
Distributing weapons to the soldiers, and powder.

9. Deli Vid will be the chief warrior fighting on Zrínyi's side.
10. The total number of troops added to Zrínyi's force, then, is 2,332.
11. I.e., 24 feet.
12. A particularly high-quality sword.

65 All types of rations and instruments of war,
Wine, bread and meat, and adequate salt,
Many picks, ladders, and all types of shovels,
Materials for building fires, and fire-extinguishing sprayers.

66 Much lumber, barrows, and flammable wood,
Saltpeter, sulfur, and burnt charcoal,
Many grenades made from hard oak;
In one word, everything that is needed for a fort, he had
brought.

67 He commands afterward: no one with the enemy
Should converse, with the pagan Turks;
For should they discover him, he will pay with his head,
And there will be for him no mercy.

68 Sentries he posts around the wall,
That this they may day and night dutifully patrol.
The many noble vajdas scurry and work;
They themselves watch over the fort.

69 When all of these Zrínyi had brought into order,
When everyone knew his own office,
According to his duty, he wrote in a letter
To the Hungarian king in such a way:

70 "It has been now two weeks, my Majestic Lord,
That the Turkish emperor has been preparing his sword
for me.
From certain of my people I heard thus,
And so unto your Highness' consideration I submitted
thus.

71 As far as I could, too, I prepared with all strength,
With my noble servants, with all sorts of armaments,

With dutiful sentries and all good order,
But the end of fortune lies with God.

72 I can write with confidence to your Highness,
That I have provided for Sziget's necessities.
If God Himself has ordered endurance unto all this,
He will keep it, who now writes to your Majesty.

73 But I fear, that another fate God has made for this fort,
And together with the fort for your faithful servant,
For they say the pagans are like gravel in their number,
And so armed even with only rocks they could bury us.

74 But if only your head be in health,
Gladly I die here in this Sziget.
I ask your Highness, that in your memory
My sons would be kept, and in grace.

75 Now I eternally bid farewell to you,
For I know, I never will see your Highness,
Therefore, may he who created the earth and heavens,
The all-powerful God, be with you."

76 Finishing the letter, he sealed it,
Then his son, György, he tenderly embraced,
Briefly, wisely, he spoke to him thus,
The child his father's words closely attended:

77 "My son, I now see you for the last time,
And for that too I bless my God,
That he allowed you to hear my final speech;
Hear, my son, I ask, my exhortation.

78 Here, in nobility I leave you,
With sword I have expanded your worth;

You will have everything; learn godly fear,
God will increase your fortune.

79 Learn from me, too, hardened chivalry,
Learn exhaustion and faithfulness to your homeland,
Learn from me good-natured action,
But from others, learn fortune and its fruits.

80 I have lived long enough already, seen evil and good,
And have now tired of meaninglessness:
For I have seen always, what the world gives
With one hand, with two it immediately jerks back.

81 I have not seen any good, in which I could rest,
I have not seen any rest, in which I could be confident;
Only in you, Jehovah, when I served,
Did I then find contentment and rest.

82 My son, serve him, and walk on that path,
Which God's son ordered upon this world,
This gives you strength over that pagan Turk,
This gives good fortune upon this earth.

83 And then remember my many trials,
Be not a bastard dove born of a fierce falcon,
Carve your fame with your sword amongst the pagans,
Let them say, that you truly were descended from Zrínyi.

84 I praise God in the heavens for you,
That he may always increase your strength;
May he grant that you would always serve his wishes,
And that in much time, in heaven you may see me.

85 This my letter take quickly to the king,
So that he may in time prepare for war,

And to attend well to the country's affairs,
For Suleiman is hurrying swiftly toward his castle."

86 "My hard-hearted father, why are you cruel?"
(Thus the young Zrínyi to the great bán responds),
"Why do you chase me from your side,
That I might be parted from you eternally?

87 Not so will I, an eagle's son, a true eagle become;
But instead a degenerate, worthless whelp,
If I from death so fearfully cower;
That which you with gladdened heart pursue, I should avoid?

88 Whatever fate God has destined to you,
It is fitting, that that same one should carry me;
With my retreat do not shame your great name;
And then for what should I save my tired-of life?

89 Is this chivalry, which you teach me,
That my first trial should be my first retreat,
That the great father's puny son should be a laughingstock?
Ah, may God not let me live to see that!

90 My lord, either leave me here with yourself,
Or I shall finish myself by my own sword;
May the Zrínyi name expire at the height of wonder,
Rather than that even one of its number should live in shame."

91 But his father answered thus with wise mind:
"Oh, great-hearted son, and full of wisdom!
As much as you swell with courage,
So much am I obliged your flame to quell.

92 For these are the thoughts of sweet honor,
But many are happily cheated thus;
There are few who can truly practice it,
Those who can couple good with a good name.

93 Reckless daring has seized you,
As the swinging branch is moved by the wind,
There will be such a time also, when in you joy
Will shine, like a beautiful flower in the garden.

94 It is not good to tear out a flower out of season,
It is not honorable for you to desire death
Now, when you could not serve anyone
With it; you must live and serve.

95 The spirit belongs not to us but God,
Will you try to wrestle over your desires with him?
Save, my son, yourself for a greater purpose,
And for our poor ruined homeland's better days.

96 It must be so, that I finish here my days,
Because God has ordered here my last hour,
Now, finally, I must show what I am made of;
Follow, when you must, my great trial."

PART SIX

1 Suleiman by now in Harsán had arrived,
The third day he rested his camp there.
From there emissaries he sent out,
To go to Zrínyi in Sziget's fortress.

2 Halul bég was the name of one of the ambassadors,
This was the son of Cairo's governor,
I say, of Orchamus, Mahomet's blood,
Who on Egypt's plain was killed by Sinan.

3 Very intelligent was Halul bég in speech,
So beautifully flowed his speech, as if mixed with honey
It were, and more subtly than the other
Did he conduct himself, and much more wisely.

4 That other was Demirham from Arabia,
Who looked as if he were from the wild plains of Libya,
One so daring and cruel there could never be;
All truth he derived only from his scimitar.

5 One more wild than he the earth could not produce;
Even if in new anger it would bring forth a giant
Who would shoot with mountains at the great heavens:
Wilder than Demirham he still would not be.

6 He was the captain of the Saracen army,
Of its fifth section, and was strong indeed,
Only for terror did the emperor him send,
Because of negotiations he knew nothing.

7 Now, these left for Szigetvár,
And when they had arrived near the gates,
At one cannon-shot's length they dismounted,
Their weapons with their servants left.

8 Zrínyi called together all the soldiers,
For he had long since heard the ambassadors;
In the square he listened to the emissaries,
Around himself stationed the knights.

9 Demirham thought little of them,
Making as if he did not see the soldiers,
But Halul put both hands on his breast,
With humility began, bowing his head:

10 "O, bright star of the followers of the faith of JESUS,
O, these knights' worthy general
Alone! What nation does not know your triumphs?
What corner of the world denies your nobility?

11 Wherefrom the warm dawn rosily deigns to arise,
Whereto in the cool evening it settles, in the ocean,
Where the North Sea churns within itself,
Your fame is everywhere, and like the sun, it shines.

12 Wonderingly, we hear of your great prowess
Everywhere; our lord also of your good fame
Enjoys hearing, and of your exploits,
He loves you also, if not your faith.

13 From such noble purpose he sent us,
To send to you, by way of us, friendship,
And to assure its endurance,
He proclaimed, by us, these sweet desires to you.

14 His desire is this: this fort into his hand
Give, and do not trust in your great endurance;
It is reckless daring, which has not strength;
Insane is he, who hopes for that which is impossible.

15 The emperor does not want your fine fort
To expand his own possessions,
Because he who commands the ends of the world
Cannot truly desire from his heart one small stone fort.

16 But you must know our end:
God's true, determined will.
To us He gives the beautiful golden apple,[1]
He polishes, too, like the sun, our crescent moon.[2]

17 Thus the mighty sultan has started now,
God's will he executes faithfully;
God forbid that you would think
That you can stay God's will with your hand.

18 O happy, wise Thamma,[3] Kazul basha's great lord!
Because from the emperor he brought himself to
 beg peace,
Quickly and shrewdly he humbled himself,
And now great Persia in peace he rules.

19 The Lusitanians[4] I hold as wise,
Because against fate, lo, they do not fight;
Lo, the French also are in bliss,
But what are you compared to these?

1. The apple or orb of state, a medieval symbol of royal rule.
2. Again, the crescent moon on the Ottoman flag and insignia.
3. The shah of Persia.
4. The Portuguese; Lusitania was the Roman province of western Iberia.

20 If you are wise, you can bring yourself good out of your need;
Do not make angry one who is greater than you:
Humble yourself, give up this fort,
Which (in no way) can you keep any longer.

21 This fort is not asked of you for free,
Where there is great profit, a little damage is unnoticeable;[5]
You may ask anything, which Emperor Suleiman
Will gladly allow, but believe you me.

22 Ask of him a command, if you do not believe,
But I know that your heart does not draw you to our faith.
Forgive me that I speak thus, because Christians,
Everyone says, are like worms fallen in horseradish.

23 Ask then much money and rich treasures,
You will not find in him any greed;
Or ask from him this fortress, Sziget,
If you love it so without reason.

24 I believe that even this he will not forbid you,
But as a sign of his rule he first desires
That his army now enter, and that one of his generals
Give it into your hand, by his command.

25 If you act otherwise, good Zrínyi,
Your fort and your men surely you will lose;
But this is nothing; your life, with your good name,
In Szigetvár's ashes will be buried.

5. A Hungarian turn of phrase; the bountiful treasury of the sultan will not miss a little of its store.

26 Perhaps there is such, who encourages you with words
of smoke,
He endangers your good name with falsehoods:
But he will be the first, who shamefully
In time of need will betray you with his flight.

27 Ticklish words are these, and all foolish!
Who will consider this nobility,
That a few stood against a hundred thousand?
Everyone will call it recklessness.

28 Perhaps your oath holds you back,
Which you made to the German emperor[6] in time
of peace?
But your conscience can now free you:
No one is obliged to do the impossible.

29 Do you have faith in the Germans, you wise Croat bán,
That they will bring you help quickly, perhaps?
The Germans, who desire that under the earth you
Would lie, would bring help to their own ruin, perhaps?

30 Who does not know of the Germans' friendship?
Especially their evil designs for the Hungarians?
Of how the German hates the Hungarian soldier,
If you wish, I can give you a thousand examples.

31 Be that as it may: arrive the Germans,
At snail's pace[7] they bring you help,
You lose then your precious lives,
And they, in Turkish hands, find Sziget.

6. Apparently the Hapsburg emperor of Austria, who controlled much of Hungary and occasionally aided in the struggle against the Ottomans.

7. In Hungarian, literally, "a crab's pace."

32 My lord, that I should tell you in one word:
Great things in a short time you have done,
National armies you have destroyed completely,
Stone fortresses you have taken, and also leveled.

33 Already your fame is at its peak;
There is no room anymore for you to take it higher,
Work only on this: that you should protect it
On that slippery place where it is; do not let it fall.

34 You must flee now from fortune's trials,
She that can break your good name's neck,
You must honorably flee, my lord, from battle,
That which can turn at any hour.

35 Let not that confidence be in your head,
That they whom you have beaten singly in battle
You can defeat now, when they are all together;
Who, by the will of God, are all gathered at your fort.

36 This, Sultan Suleiman who loves you,
Has told you, Zrínyi, through us.
Here he comes himself too; a nation of one million
He brings for your ruin, if you ignore his word."

37 Here Halul fell silent, and there fell a clamor
Amongst the strong knights, and disquiet;
Well knows Halul, that it is wearisome for them,
Such treating and the fort's surrender.

38 The Croat bán looked over his many good knights,
Then turned his eye on the ambassadors;
All are silent, await the bán's pleasure;
He, with great dignity, began his speech:

39 "Good ambassador, wisely you have explained to us,
Softly, and with anger too, your lord's message;
With pleasant words you have emphasized your lord's love,
Which he brings to us, and his good humor.

40 I wonder, because I did not intend
To find mercy with your emperor;
In fact, I have hurt him, out of my small ability,
Wherever I could, and with all my powers.

41 Of my friendship too I speak briefly:
Never can I be a friend to a Turk,
As long as I see that he hurts Christians;
Friendship, harm cannot fit together.

42 But if my friendship the emperor craves,
It can be so; the Magyars' possessions he may give back,
And afterward not desire other Christians';
Then, perhaps I can be his friend.

43 Whereas you ask for Szigetvár in his name,
Good ambassador, you must know that which I tell you,
That Zrínyi has suffered much with these men:
Evil, peril, cold, and heat,

44 So that we could win favor with God;
Therefore we do not consider the loss of our lives,
Many treasures, wealth, and our everything,
And this mortal worldly fame.

45 Then let not the emperor soothe us with these;
These, which we leave to the world with great joy.
If he believes not our word, let him come upon us with force,
He will see what this man can do: this man who is with God.

46 But if for our sins God us
Thrashes, and gives into your hands our lives:
We die gladly, but you our loss
Will not rejoice over, nor the Christians'.

47 We therefore do not envy your lives either;
We gladly depart Sziget for the heavens.
Take to your emperor my speech;
Suleiman will see, too, what Zrínyi can do."

48 Demirham cannot tolerate Zrínyi's speech,
Because the harsh reply has pierced through his heart;
Says: "O, you! who ignore battle's danger,
And think that you have caught fortune by its tail![8]

49 Here are both war and peace in my breast,
Now choose for yourself, while you still have time,
Because I don't understand, in flowery speech;
You meander, and switch between war, peace."

50 To such words the armies rise up,
They do not wait the answer of powerful Zrínyi,
"Arms! Arms!" they cry to the emissaries;
"With arms, not with words must Sziget be defeated."

51 "Then to deadly weapons I call you!"
Answers Demirham: "for I see your lives
Bore you." With such a voice did he say these,
As if Janus's temple had opened just now.[9]

52 Quickly it falls into the ear of the emperor,
That Zrínyi, together with the others, stands in great
defiance.

8. The word "tail" here implies a comet's tail.

9. The Temple of Janus in ancient Rome was traditionally closed during peacetime and opened during times of war.

He does not delay long, leaps in his great rage
Against Zrínyi and Sziget, and in great pride.

53 Sokolovich Mehmet he called to himself,
Him with hot anger commanded
That in the entire camp he should blow reveille,
And that Osman basha he should put in the lead.

54 And with Osman basha Ali Kurtog[10] should go:
He, great Asia's beglerbeg,
And on water, on land, the emperor's chief artillery sergeant;
He commanded, that with him twenty hundred janissaries would go;

55 And that they would encircle Sziget's surroundings,
They would see, where there would be a place to launch siege,
Wherefrom they could invincibly attack Sziget,
Whereto the cavalry and janissaries could move their corps;

56 And that he himself tomorrow, in the first of beautiful dawn
Should depart and follow in Osman's path.
Then left Osman in that same hour,
For he does not dare to miss anything by his delay.

57 The beglerbeg takes ten thousand swords unto himself,
Ali Kurtog is with two thousand janissaries,
The Turkish army proceeds in good order;
The sentry gave a signal in Sziget with his bell.

58 Zrínyi a mounted team dispatched from the fortress,
So that of the Turks' intentions it could bring news.

10. Ali Kurt plays a prominant role in the epic as the master of the sultan's cannons.

Fortune into their hands a Turk gave,
Who, toward the fortress, from the others broke away.

59 This gave away to them the beglerbeg's intention,
And that tomorrow he awaited the emperor's camp,
Quickly opened Zrínyi the gates,
Brought out with himself twelve hundred swords.

60 The basha had bedded down by now in a great mill,
Where the grassy Almás flows with slow roar,
Across the water is Ali Kurt with half his forces;
They seek: in what fashion to ruin Szigetvár.

61 The Turks the horses all send out to graze,
Here and there themselves also recline everywhere,
The fools cannot even call to each other,
They do not fear that the Christians would come upon them.

62 Between the fortress and the Turks there was a small hill,
Therefore the Turks did not see the Christians;
But as soon as good Zrínyi went up on the hill,
A Turk named Dervish saw him there.

63 He cries, "Lo, infidel!" He does not cry for long,
Because upon him lunges Dandó, like a furious dragon,
He thrust his sword into Dervish to his armpit,
From his life, from his voice, he is once and for all divorced.

64 Shouting, rushing, upon the camp descend;
One chases his horse, another upon his horse leaps;
He, however, into trenches shamefully hides;
Even the basha himself there is terrified.

65 Have you seen ants when upset?
With all speed here and there they scurry,

The wretched ones their great eggs carry:
Likewise these now dart, vainly, in all directions.

66 But Sziget's captain does not much delay,
Amongst them bravely like a knight he lunges.
There where in groups the Turks congregate,
By Zrínyi's hand quickly they are dispersed.

67 Perhaps thus dealt Hercules with the dragons,[11]
Or mighty Samson with the Philistines,[12]
As Zrínyi does with Turkish pagans,
With a hard and sharp Fringian sword.

68 With this he took the life of Ramadan,
He separated Jusup's head from his body,
And that of Karaman Nuh, Persian Assagur,
Torlak, Dedo, massive-bodied Halul.[13]

69 Of no use is to you a fake amulet,
Murtuzanogli, Murtuzan basha's son,
Nor to you holiness, Balukbis Yahia,
All are laid under the ground by the Fringian.

70 Deli Vid elsewhere amongst the Turks, like an avenging spirit,
A hundred with his spear with great strength beats down,
By now his clothes are nothing but Turkish blood;
Alone among them, like a lion, he dares to tread.

11. Hercules killed Draco, a hundred-headed dragon, with one spear throw.

12. Samson, a warrior for the Israelites when they were being oppressed by the Philistines, toppled the pillars of their temple with God-given strength while they were feasting inside, killing over a thousand. Cf. Judges 16.

13. Apparently not the ambassador Halul.

71 I cannot even call this a battle or a skirmish,
But a terrible, horrific bloodbath,
For Turks everywhere, like dust, fly,
Some on horse, some on foot, some into trenches run.

72 Died Kara Illan at Radován's hand,
Tarluk oda-basha from Novák's great wound;
Saracen Gisdaris from his weapon
Lies, biting the earth miserably.

73 Across the Almás creek is the janissary corps,
But there cannot be any help from them,
For the water's height reaches the throat of a man,
Their weapons will soak, if they come across.[14]

74 The basha vainly calls to them thus:
"Indeed, you are the traitors to the Turkish emperor
If to us help you do not speedily bring:
Not true Turks, but Turkish traitors."

75 Ali Kurt gladly would bring help,
But he knew well the water's depth:
A horse cannot overcome the great, steep riverbed,
And a footman will drench all his weapons.

76 Still, though it was dark, into the river the janissaries
Start to wade, like so many thick reeds;
Their guns in their hands they hold high aloft,
So that in the Almás's waters they would not soak.

77 Help they wish to bring to the retreaters,
But goes before them deathbringer Zrínyi,

14. The janissaries, famous for their musket skills, risked soaking their powder if they waded into the river.

Having waded into the water to his waist;
There he begins to cut them wrathfully.

78 "Whereto have you started, you despicable curs?"
(Thus shouts Sziget's captain to the Turks),
"For, indeed, that I myself will come to you;
Here I am, search for me no longer."

79 Lightning crashes quickly where the sky roars:
Zrínyi after these words immediately falls to them;
There by him Kurt aga is killed from one wounding,
From another, Toigon's head is taken.

80 There is no such Damascan sword, which does not break
in two,
Before Zrínyi's hand many heads are felled;
As if walking only through reeds, so walks he,
Because those many Turks flee, fall, and are wounded.

81 Already piles are before him of dead bodies,
The Almás's water also fills with these,
Every last drop of water is made of black blood;
Flee the Turks, along with their fleeing leader.

82 Osman quickly swam his horse across the river,
Zrínyi, too, was separated from the battle by nightfall.
His army smartly he regrouped,
Slowly he departed with them for Sziget.

83 But valiant Deli Vid went across the river,
Upon the rear of the Turks,[15] and bringing more death.
In front of him goes Hamvivan the Saracen,
He recognized Vid by his fine weapon.

15. This can also be read as: "Deli Vid crossed the river on the backs of Turkish corpses."

84 With little force he cast his spear at him,
It connected with the center of Vid's great shield,
It lost its strength, having found a greater power than itself,
The spear falls to the ground, blunted.

85 Young Hamvivan grew scared in his heart,
He no longer has hope in an unarmed hand,
He ran away from Vid, lighter than wind,
He trusts in the great speed of his flight.

86 But quickly Vid chases after him, mercilessly,
In a few leaps reached him suddenly,
He spoke thus: "It seems that you are a sly Saracen:
You trust more in your feet, and not in your weapon.

87 But you won't be served by your homeward flight,
This iron will now tear your heart."
After these words he cast upon him a mighty javeline throw,
Of which high heaven had never seen an equal.

88 His leaden shield Hamvivan held up,
But through it the mighty iron lance ripped,
On Hamvivan's belt there was a great round stone mace,
That too, the deadly spear crushed into dust.

89 It went through his stomach also, nor did his back stay
the blow,
Because his precious life it tore out;
Falls down Hamvivan before Vid, collapsed,
Into the ground he was nailed by Deli Vid's spear.

90 With speed Deli Vid charges upon him, and his lance
He yanked out of his gut, bracing himself with his foot.
The Turks hear Deli Vid's merciless words;
Standing above the Turk, thus he opened his throat:

91 “That which you have sought by force, here at Szigetvár,
I give to you beautiful Pannonia;
But lie down now, like a measuring rod:
You Saracen brat, measure its breadth.”

92 Like a wild lion having killed its prey,
Contemptuously strutting his rage over it,
With his cruel eyes he watches its agonies,
He glories in blood, he washes his mane:

93 So likewise Deli Vid stood atop the Turk,
His lance in his hand like a great oak beam,
He can be seen well in the distance, like a straight stone wall;
He watches, where he may find new foes.

94 Hamvivan’s weapon he peacefully removed,
His gold-woven shirt he also donned himself,
But Kamber did not tolerate this for long,
With such a loud voice he screamed to the army:

95 “O, shamed ones! You are knights?
Thus we show shame on the first day to Sziget?
Your eyes see noble, dead Hamvivan;
One man killed him, you let him be killed.

96 To plunder his corpse you allow,
And you watch an infidel dancing upon him;
Where are now your boasting hearts,
Where at home did you leave your tossed and abused
courage?

97 But foresaw this the great Menetham,
When this his son he sent into the Turkish army;
Often with great tears he shouted in farewell:
‘Be safe my son, my fair son, Hamvivan!

98 Do not be self-assured in Turkish unity,
Many nations, many good soldiers have been disappointed
by it;
Never will a Turk help you in battle,
Believe him, but then you will never return to Syria.'

99 Often to me also the great king shouted,
Commending his son to me he often asked:
'Kamber, my sweet servant, guide my son,
Who was seized by his desire for the Turkish army!'

100 But I cannot desire my return,
But by my lord's side I will lose my life,
Menetham will see my faithfulness,
Though now too late, my great and true heart."

101 Thus he says, and no more: from his servant a lance
He grabs, and searches for Zrínyi's lieutenant.
Fears not Deli Vid, but stiffly his lance
In his great hand holds and nourishes his fury.

102 But at Kamber's words, the entire Turkish force,
Everyone in his own heart is moved by sorrow;
Once and for all, Deli Vid they surround,
So that other than his own hands, there is no hope.

103 But Vid, like a stone cliff, stands amidst the foam,
Valorously he stands against the fog of war,
His shield is filled with a great gust of weaponry,
Arrows, spears, scimitars fly densely above his head.

104 Like a howling demon, Kamber goes upon Vid,
So that for his lord he might exact revenge,
A Syrian reed-shafted lance he hurls at him powerfully,
But astounded, sees it broken on the ground.

105 Kurt aga with a fine dagger wounded him,
But only barely bloodied his head,
Ibraim his scimitar broke on Vid's shield,
Ali Kurt with his lance hit him in the side.

106 Kamber from his sheath immediately draws his sword,
Mercilessly pounds Deli Vid's helmet,
Then Deli Vid thrusted at him his spear,
But the spear did not do its lord's will

107 Because Kamber lept aside, but neither did it pass
empty-handed,
That cruel cornel-tree; but mercilessly,
It pierces the center of Zizim aga's breast,
For which his life dissipates into the air.

108 Zizim lies on the ground due to a foreign wound;
Deli Vid draws his man-killing scimitar.
With one blow he kills angry Kurt aga,
With the other Kamber, Hamvivan's servant.

109 Kamber with sweet death fell beside his lord,
With many bloody gasps his life flew away,
Of his blood and loyalty at once his body cooled;
One more faithful than he a mother never bore.

110 Vid finds a way for himself with his scimitar,
Like a consuming fire he passes, aflame,
So that from amongst them he emerges with fury,
He strides toward the water, soaked with blood and dust.

111 The Turkish forces do not follow him,
But rather, rejoice that he went out from among them;
But he anxiously set out toward the water;
That he came out from among them, he counts as shame.

112 Three times he stopped in the Almás creek,
He will go back upon them, he thinks to himself,
But he sees Zrínyi, that he is in formation,
And that they are all waiting on him.

113 Weapons and all he jumps into the Almás,
And the Almás carries him on its back,
And its flow washed him of the pagan blood,
Thus it sent him to his lord and companions, cleansed.

114 Together with good Zrínyi he goes into Sziget,
And all the knights are rejoicing;
Vid glories in Hamvivan's weapon,
Who, in life, was the Syrian king's son.

115 Three thousand cavalry were lost in this skirmish,
Five hundred janissaries lie in the Almás creek;
But greater loss than all of these is Hamvivan,
Who by Vid's lance lies pinned to the ground.

PART SEVEN

1 Once dawn's graceful chariot
Had moved all things to beauty,
Sweet nightingale to bitter song,
And the knights of Sziget to great joy,

2 Quickly arrived the news in the emperor's camp:
Zrínyi had defeated Osman basha in a great battle,
Lost his life and arms Hamvivan,
Lost his dear son basha Murtuzan.

3 This fell into the ear of wild Demirham,
For which his heart was moved to painful sorrow;
Senselessly he rends his own clothes,
As if by this he could help Hamvivan.

4 "Where have you left me, Menetham's great son?"
(For his father's very close friend was he,
And Hamvivan he lamented with harsh throat),
"How did this happen, that your soul has gone below under the earth?

5 Is this what I swore to my friend,
The Syrian king, your father,
That in battle I should abandon you,
And give you up as prey to the sword of the infidels?

6 But who is guilty in this? Only you, fool,
That you would charge out from among us so suddenly;
No one knew this in your battalion,
Only your servant Kamber, also an unfortunate.

7 But may Hamvivan's soul be to me gracious,
Because for you there will soon be vengeance,
Your executioner's soul will be eaten by iron,
I swear to Mahomet, whose soul the great sky holds aloft.

8 Your bloody heart I will take to Menetham,
Though his sorrow it will not much quell;
Therefore I will take revenge on all of Sziget,
And wherever I find them, all Christians."

9 With such words strode Demirham to the emperor,
And when he came close to the emperor's tent,
The emperor saw in his eyes that he brought ill tidings;
Demirham began speaking thus to Suleiman:

10 "We pointlessly rest ourselves here,
Sziget's bán beat your army over there;
The infidels killed Hamvivan, my comrade,
And Murtazan's son, and Osman they humiliated.

11 My padishah,[1] either give me leave alone,
That I may fulfill my wrathful vengeance upon them,
Or let you yourself bring your camp,
Ruin those faithless pagan infidels."

12 Demirham's temper the emperor knew,
Therefore to defy him there he did not dare.
"Here and now we depart," he replied him,
"Hamvivan was your companion, take vengeance for him."

13 So set out Suleiman with his camp,
With precise military order;

1. A title of royalty, literally "high king." "Basha" is actually a contraction of "padishah," but the latter was applied exclusively to sultans.

Arrived at Szigetvár that same day
At two in the afternoon with his great camp.

14 Also watching Sziget's tower was Zrínyi;
Sees from afar—climbs to the top—
Horrendously thick dust, which was thrown into the sky,
So that earth and sky were both darkened.

15 Late they saw those many Turks,
Likewise a dark cloud in the air.
For the earth was blanketed by the masses,
As if a mountain were moving over a level plain.

16 Above the armies a huge dust cloud swirls,
Below them with great terror the earth trembles,
Many thousands of crimson banners in the wind flutter,
You would think, that now even the sea was crashing upon you.

17 The world-destroying camp laid siege around the fortress,
Like massive ice sheets locked in the Danube.
Everywhere was displayed the white of many countless tents;
They were afraid of no one, brave in their strength.

18 The emperor inspected the fortress from all around,
Afterward he himself encamped beyond a hill,
Then the entire camp "Allahu" cried
Once after another, three times, then finally stopped.

19 The entire janissary corps in ordered rank,
Guns in each one's destructive hands—
These each shot into the sky,
For the emperor's arrival are they so overjoyed.

20 But the cannons they also at once discharged,
You would think high heavens are collapsing upon you;
Below the earth trembles, cracks like ice,
Sziget's keep is moved by fright.

21 Zrínyi leaves it to the artillerymen
To give the Turks a greeting from the cannons.
First Csontos Pál one end of the fuse
Inserts into the hole of the wolfcannon.[2]

22 Quickly the terrific gun discharges,
Toward the Turkish camp sends a hail of bullets;
Invisibly, shot flies into the midst of the forces,
Horrific deaths it brings to them,

23 Because first it found the janissary-aga's head,
Turban and all it ended his life,
After him, thirty-nine bodies in a row;
It cruelly wrecks the warrior Turks.

24 Glad is Csontos Pál, that he caused such,
To the Turks from the bastion he loudly calls:
"Here is your greeting cup, you are well-come,
I'll give to him also, who has not yet drunk.

25 From Szigetvár will come such greetings:
You have strong stomachs, digest them.
You will not come into Sziget if you do not drink them:
To Zrínyi's health, treacherous Turkish curs."

26 Pál with the second shot Aigas basha's
Horse shredded, and Pécsi Dezdar's
Chest, and also twenty-three others;
They sprawl on the ground and expel their souls.

2. A stationary cannon made for fortress defenses.

27 But the third shot they do not dare await,
They hurry to shelter, each to flee;
Some cannot find his own
In his great fright, and does not dare halt.

28 With two shots, great harm befell the Turks;
Much greater now happened in Sziget,
For Farkasics Péter in his old injury
Prepares his soul to go before God;[3]

29 And he is only worried that he would die in bed.
Foolish is he, the will of the living God
With complaints he cannot deflect.
Before the knights he complains thus:

30 "Hey, hey, how cruel is my fate!
Of this in all my years I was terrified,
That shamefully in bed, I my life would send
Into the almighty merciful God's hand.

31 O, a thousand times are they glad who beside their
homeland
Nobly laid down their lives,
Fortune however kept me for this,
That uselessly I would expend my life.

32 Ah, unfortunate me, I could not die,
Where with sweet death died great Losonci,[4]

3. Apparently the author made a mistake, combining two historical persons named "Farkasics"; the one dying here is the one who was hurt earlier, while the one who led his forces into Sziget, "healed of his old wound," was never actually wounded in the first place.

4. István Losonczy; died in 1552 when he surrendered the fortress of Temesvárto to the Turks and was betrayed.

Where lies Rácz Milák and Farkas Bottyáni,[5]
Noble Spaniard Perez, old Kastelánfi![6]

33 But could not I from great Dragut's hand,
Or vicious Akomat's fine weapon
Be divorced from this, my insipid life?
Here and now must I die without glory!

34 When I was pressed by twenty arrows,
When I fell to earth from Gyafer's lance,
When I was mortally wounded by Rahmat's club,
My life was preserved, and now it leaves from my bed!

35 But it is good, if it is so, for it is God's will;
Often his faithful servant he harshly whips,
So that in the heavens he would crown him more radiantly,
For his suffering amply reward him.

36 Here, my noble friends, now I die,
To you good fortune from God I go to implore,
In the skies on your behalf the good God I will praise,
Be soldiers; now God be with you!"

37 Thus Farkasics Péter ended his life,
To God he sent his pure noble soul,
Mourns good Zrínyi his passing;
With great emotion he began his speech thus:

38 "O, spinning fate, accursed, cruel!
Why have you seized this knight so suddenly?
This was lacking in our wretchedness,
That Farkasics would not be here alive.

5. Two more defenders of Temesvár.

6. Alonso Perez and Gaspar Castellnuovo, commanders of Spanish mercenaries at Temesvár.

39 O, life, how soon you dissipate from this earth!
O, short life, how quickly you fly from us!
When we need you the most, you cease,
And, as dew before the sun, once and for all disappear.

40 As dew before the sun, as snow before the fire,
Like a dream before us, like smoke before the wind,
Or like a swift cyclone as it drives the clouds,
So you disappear before us and before our dreams.

41 Wickedly slithers the vile snake on the meadow,
Nothing does it care for its dull aging,
It rejuvenates, whenever it cares to,
It throws away its old skin and is renewed in its body:

42 Man, however, he who in God's image
Is made, in God's resemblance,
If arrives his last hour,
Does not return and does not renew, but goes to his death.

43 Ages the earth, loses its beauty,
But it renews, if it reaches the time of Spring;
The sun finishes daily its round,
But it is renewed in the morning, bringing forth its chariot.

44 Only wretched man is alone,
Who from quick-arriving senility does not return;
In permanent surge is the eternal fresh river,
In man, however, blood never renews.

45 Water, fire, earth, and great sky last for long:
Man, lord of these, for the blink of an eye;
Stone walls, great towers for many hundreds of years:
Man, who made these, for an hour.

46 There is only one which lives beyond the grave,
That which shows itself when the world is in need:
A noble deed, having great eternity;
It is renewed in every age, for it cannot die.

47 Renews, Farkasics, your noble name,
Though the heavy earth covers your body.
By your deeds you defeated death,
Now at God's right hand is your glory.

48 There now is repaid your work in life,
Gleefully the angels examine your scars;
There, your blood which you spilled for your homeland,
The saints convert to eternal happiness."

49 So Zrínyi buried Farkasics,
Then concerned himself with every part of the fortress;
Sziget's soldiers are in silence,
Everywhere on the towers, on guard.

50 The Turks were entrenched now all around,
Everywhere the many Turks were glad for the nice weather,
Only Suleiman himself in grave concerns is graying,
The bán's daring soul cools him with fear.

51 The bán of Sziget does not long delay,
His heart is made braver, seeing the enemy;
Like the terrible Armenian lion
He emerges from his cave, seeing arms outside:

52 Thus goes Zrínyi from Sziget upon the Turks,
Powerful man-killing lance is in his hand,
The wind flutters the light ostrich feather on his head;
Five hundred knights follow him in proud ranks,

53 He turned to them, thus he called to his army:
"Hear what I say, you valiant knights,
The first day, the first battle will now be before us,
Today we must put fear into the Turkish dogs.

54 Today, we will make the Turkish emperor understand
What are our hearts, our hands, our weapons.
Today we must make ourselves terrible;
So, my noble servants, be men."

55 With few words the bán gave great courage
To his valorous forces, which can hardly wait,
That all the sooner they could be face to face with the Turks;
If it were allowed, they would immediately run to the fray.

56 Not far from the fort, Ali Kurt toils,
He has made all the preparations for trench digging;
Rushtan, the sultan's son-in-law, brings five thousand janissaries,
Settles them not far from Ali Kurt.

57 But Stipán Golemi, good Zrínyi's lieutenant,
Leads the soldiers there on patrol,
With great bravery strikes there upon the asaps,[7]
Those who are digging trenches, along with the janissaries.

58 Many Turks fall because of those hundred infantry,
For not one fires uselessly his carbine;
But in order, the janissary corps beats itself into a strong wall,
Prepares its weapons, guns, and fuses.

7. An irregular infantry force, often used for digging trenches.

59 Rechep janissary-aga the first division
Brings to bear upon Stipán vajda, his fiery armaments,
But Stipán Golemi is not fazed by him,
He watches his enemy, and like an oak, stands before the wind.

60 The Turk foolishly discharges his gun,
Stipán spied out Rechep janissary-aga,
Bravely brought upon him his double-edged broadsword,
Smashed it to his head, slicing his turban.

61 On his two shoulders falls from two directions his head,
With great clamor he fell himself on the ground,
But from Stipán's hand more also fell beside him,
For Abaz, Benavir, and Mustapha he killed.

62 Rushtan bég set out with five thousand janissaries,
To where Stipán vajda was doing damage with his broadsword,
Zrínyi to Golemi with four hundred good swords
In time brings help, with order.

63 He whom the Lord God wishes to uphold,
Even among a hundred thousand will stand.
By five thousand guns could not be killed
Anyone in the army, in which was good Zrínyi.

64 As soon as the smoke dissipated, with great howling
Captain Rushtan charged with his many janissaries;
The five thousand men stand in three battalions,
Mercilessly entangled with the bán's legion.

65 You were the first, great Croat Radivoj,
Who spilled pagan Turkish blood with your scimitar,

Fell before you in cruel death
Pervis oda-basha, the ambidextrous.

66 But soon after him Juranics Lőrinc
Achomat flag-bearer with his sword cut down;
Before Zrínyi already fifteen dead are sprawled,
On top of Turkish bodies he strides, wading in blood.

67 Arslan, Rushtan's brother, recognized Zrínyi,
Daringly with his lance upon him wrecked,
Breaks his lance, and uselessly on the ground
It fell, because its tip collided with the shield.

68 Quickly the young Arslan drew sword;
The Croat bán holds before him his shield,
He has taken now two blows, but not awaiting more,
Strikes with his scimitar, trusting in its strength.

69 With ruthless scimitar he cleaves his chest in two,
His still-living heart inside was beating;
He pales, like a delicate violet
At Zrínyi's feet he falls.

70 From his opened chest red blood spews,
In his body, life struggles with death,
Finally his life is trumped by death,
His soul slips from his body on a wide avenue.[8]

71 But Sanzak Benavir does not frighten from this;
In his hand he grips his powerful, keen dagger,
He goes thence, where Zrínyi is wrecking Arslan bég,
And thus proudly begins his speech:

8. "Wide avenue" here may be taken both as a reference to the ease by which the soul escaped, that is, the size and severity of the wound; and also as the opposite to the biblical "narrow way," which would imply his soul went to hell.

72 "You have emerged from your hole, false and treacherous fox,
You will not return there, though you are laden with intelligence.
Your feet were made to flee, and this spot the grave
Will be for your treacherous corpse, and this hour its last.

73 But with what torture shall I kill you?
For Arslan's slaughter your beating heart—
It will not be enough for me to devour, or the dogs
Well to feed with it, having destroyed your body.

74 But here your executioner will be this dagger,
A worthy punishment it will extract from your heart."
With such words he wrathfully charges at Zrínyi,
Stabs at him, but Zrínyi jumps aside suddenly.

75 "Perhaps a better blow is this, which comes from my hand,
For it is stronger, and it comes from a more worthy person."
Thus responds Zrínyi, with his scimitar valiantly
Striking his waist; and seeing his blood, he is happy.

76 Benavir falls, and his soul gurgles in his throat;
In his fall his weapon loudly clatters.
See the hand "made for fleeing," Turkish cur,
It laid you out on the ground; lay here forever!

77 Does not hesitate Deli Vid, seeing his valiant lord,
But amidst all those Turks, he broke his lance.
Lays before him Kayradin Kayrakat,
He killed Hussein, Al, Cefer, Mustapha.

78 Here courage took the Christian host,
The Turk however trembles with fear.

Joza Pál took the life of Bichir,
Penezics Ábrahám those of Nuh and Deriel.

79 Tamburás Istók also threw Toigan to the ground,
Strong Dandó Iván Ibrahim killed;
Juranics killed Barjaktar with his carbine,
His gilded flag took from his hand.

80 But I do not know, from whence Demirham arrives,
For cries from the battle fall in his ear,
Swiftly among the warriors he arrives,
Sees that the Turks are ready for fleeing.

81 With Tamburás Istók he sees the Turkish flag,
For Juranics to him gave it, to carry,
"Not for you, infidel dog, is meant the glorious banner!"
From afar to Istók, Demirham cries.

82 Along with such words to him, he drew his sword;
Istók in his fright threw aside the banner.
Into his hand, too, there came a sword,
With untrained hand he struck him with it.

83 Demirham took up the blow with his scimitar,
Indeed, struck him with the same motion,
Which on his flank made a grave wound,
Through that his life exited, and into him flew death.

84 Demirham dismounted his steed for the flag,
But as soon as he saw the feathered Deli Vid,
Nimbly, like a squirrel, immediately he leapt astride his horse,
Gave the flag into another Turk's hands.

85 This is that Demirham, who that day in Sziget
Went before Zrínyi with such anger.

Now again a spear he took into his destructive hand;
He proves ferocity in his actions.

86 Like the furious dragon, he springs on Vid,
But the fierce lance breaks on the shield.
But Vid's pike fell into the horse's head,
For which the horse along with its lord fell.

87 Instantly and lightly Demirham, like a quick ferret,
Left his horse on the ground and drew his weapon,
He lunges at Deli Vid, staring bravely into his eyes,
As if he did not even see enemies elsewhere.

88 "What are you waiting for?" said Deli Vid,
"Indeed, I have waited for you thus long, until you
clambered up
From under the horse: my hands have work to do elsewhere,
Not just with you." Demirham gave answer thus:

89 "With your sword you goad me upon yourself,
Because I do not recognize you, looking at you;
Perhaps Deli Vid I would identify you,
You who Hamvivan's life took away.

90 But whoever you may be, you will have no more worries,
For today my hand will give you your fill,
My sword upon you for Turkish blood will take revenge,
Therefore, for such short time, let not your heart fret."

91 "I am Deli Vid," replies the other,
"But why do you blather, your mouth babbling?
Because of my hand Hamvivan lies here,
And by it, your head will fall to the ground."

92 Demirham, like a demon, upon hearing this,
That because of this one's hand occurred his friend's death,

Great Damascan sword he heaves in his hand,
Thus he goes in great wrath upon Deli Vid.

93 Like two infuriated Libyan lions,
Running together on the great wide plain,
They try their claws on each others' furred backs:
So the two warriors do on Szigetvár's border.

94 Demirham in anger and wrath is greater,
But Deli Vid in the true faith is braver;
They allow each other no quarter, the swords spark,
The strong steel covering them from great distance shines.

95 Turk in two blows Deli Vid's shield
Breaks in pieces, but Turk's helmet
Deli Vid crushes, because his scimitar's flat
He smashes to the helmet, wounding his forehead.

96 These fight thus, but the rest of the forces
Of strong Zrínyi's hand grew afraid.
Benavir's army was the first to flee,
Afterward Arslan's, having lost their lord.

97 Started Rushtan also, have grown afraid of the affair,
He does not think to take vengeance for his brother on
 Zrínyi;
Zrínyi chases the Turks back on their own trails,
Everywhere, Christian swords are at their backs.

98 He chases them, but wisely, because he sees from afar,
That many thousand cavalry are coming to his harm:
For the powerful Deliman, the great Tatar khan's son,
Like a lion cub is coming upon Zrínyi's men.

99 The bán, when he saw that great mass,
His dispersed army he there gathered,

For now the radiant sun also had driven off its horses
Into the ocean-sea; it was also dark.

100 Rushtan would hardly have escaped with his many infantry,
If Deliman would not have arrived with his many cavalry.
But fights Demirham even now with Deli Vid,
They cannot cause each other any harm with swords.

101 When it was dark, Demirham said thus:
"We here, like the blind, are foolishly exhausting
Ourselves pointlessly, and we cannot with sword hurt
Each other; will it not be better to fight by day?

102 By day, then, the jealous darkness our work
Cannot hide, for the sky will see,
Szigetvár will see, and the Turkish army,
What powerful revenge inflicts upon you Demirham bég.

103 Therefore swear to me on God,
I, too, will swear on Mahomet's faith:
That you too will return, as will I, to this place,
As soon as you, and I, have means to do so.

104 For because of darkness we can now no longer fight,
But I believe, we may still have opportunity,
For I know, we from here will not quickly leave,
Until you all from the walls we do not cleave out."

105 Answers Deli Vid: "To give a flowery speech
I would like, but I have not a way
To know with certainty that I may come out,
And to thus put forth my life against the great army.

106 But believe you this, if I could know with certainty,
That my foe would be Demirham alone,

Never would I hide from him behind a stone wall,
But in forest, on meadow, anywhere I would await him."

107 "Do not fear, Deli Vid, for your life from others,
For I will bring you from the emperor a letter,
Demirham alone will be your opponent,
Suleiman will give his true Turkish word."

108 Thus to mortal danger they swear.
Then quickly from each other they separate,
Like two wild forest-bulls,[9]
Who with antlers cannot harm each other.

9. Deer.

PART EIGHT

1 Here comes on winged horse the graceful red dawn,
Its bridle washes in white foam,
The horse was black, but more beautiful than Pegasus,
From it nostril comes fire, from its eye, death.

2 A small white cambric cloth covers his head,
But his face shines in full radiance,
He himself is dressed in a golden mail shirt,
Two ebony lances are in his shining hands.

3 Every tiny bit of sweat which drips from the horse
On the ground becomes pretty frail dew,
Before him darkness in full retreat is dissipating,
Around him the sky from afar is twinkling.

4 With his youthful face to all he brings joy,
He draws forth flowers from the earth with his beauty,
He opens the mournful throat of the nightingale,
He stream, river, forest, meadow rejuvenates.

5 And when he arrives above Szigetvár,
He falls into such dubious thoughts:
"Lo, how many corpses lie in this place.
The sky is hidden by a great air of stench.

6 I wonder whose handiwork this could be?
Perhaps here a plague, or dragon could be?
It has ruined the Magyars' beautiful land:
Perhaps evil Python[1] has again awoken?

1. A mythical dragon, killed by Apollo.

7 If that, then I will climb down to earth from high heaven,
With my two sharp spears I will save from the venom
Of the dragon the Magyars, and from danger.
But, it seems to me, I see a camp there off to the side.

8 Ah, the faithless Turk I see in the plain!
This more than the dragon I despise in my heart.
Ah, faithless curs, if it were in my power,
All of you I would waste in my wrathful humor.

9 But it is well, for I see, they do not greatly rejoice;
In fact, with great laments they howl into the sky.
Give not, give not fortune, God, to these!
Allow that by Magyar hands they would be wasted, to a
man!

10 Blessed be you, good Zrínyi, who thus ruins them,
And you who faithless corpses pile in heaps,
After all, your homeland awaits all fortune from you alone;
Therefore, and for your own glory, spare not your life."

11 But Suleiman grows grayer in his massive camp,
His heart is chilled by worries and is in great sorrow.
Zrínyi has showed him now twice in two battles,
What he can further hope for in Pannonia.

12 "What can I await further" (thus he begins to complain),
"In whom can I trust, and who must I believe?
Here my father's spirit was ready to deceive me,
Said he, that Suleiman in Sziget will live.

13 It was not enough for my father to deceive me:
The prophet Mahomet himself lied to me,
That in my hand will be my fine gold apple,
And that under me, the Muslim will rule the world.

14 Thus I have triumphed over the whole world,
Weeping, it beseechingly brought me tribute,
My mighty weapon reigned over the whole world,
Where rose, where set the sun, it feared my sword.

15 Trembled before me the great Emperor Charles,
Because of me fell Uluduveidar,[2]
In wide Egypt, I suffered little loss:
What fraction of these powers is this thieves' hideout?[3]

16 The world-ruling emperor is defeated by Zrin,
Here I wasted all my strength upon him,
Here is the janissary corps, my terrible army,
It is lost once and for all at his hand.

17 There is none more deft than Demirham in the world,
But what has he harmed Zrínyi in these two battles?
Black Hamvivan lies on the Almás shore,
Did not wise Rushtan walk just yesterday?

18 See the Tatar khan's son, wrathful Deliman:
We thought of him that he was a roaring lion;
Disappears his bravery, if out comes the Croat bán,
He does not hurry there to battle, where Zrínyi is.

19 Ah, ah, if only you were not alive, valorous Zrínyi bán!
If I had not tripped over you in conquest;
Like Alexander the Great, you would be great, Suleiman,
But lo, how I must suffer, spending myself here!"

20 World-wrecking Suleiman broke his heart thus,
For his wise chief advisors he quickly sent,

2. An honorific.

3. The Hungarian word here, *szarkavár,* literally means "magpie castle." Though no longer in use in Hungarian, it referred to a fortification on a national border, from which soldiers could launch pillaging raids into other countries.

Sokolovich Mehmet these collected,
In the emperor's tent he had them orderly sit.

21 But the emperor does not wish to sit down amongst them,
So that his transformation no one would notice;
From a hidden tent he watched the council.
Sokolovich Mehmet began his speech thus:

22 "Noble lords, triumphant wise chiefs,
Beglerbegs from the corners of the world,
You bashas, you begs, you cunning generals,
Who now in this place have gathered to council!

23 The mighty emperor, Sultan Suleiman khan,
Whom the moon serves, who has claim over
Ocean and sea, who is under the sky;
In this place, desires to live by your advice.

24 He desires to hear, therefore, from you,
What means are needed to destroy this Sziget
Without harm and Turkish blood, and that time's
Length would not hurt his great name.

25 Each of your councils, written down, he has ordered,
I should bring unto his hand, so that he could see
What is most needed to serve the Turks,
What to do in this infidel-destroying army.

26 To remind you, he commanded me,
Of this council's foremost task,
That we have come upon the strongest infidel in the world
Who girds a sword to his side.[4]

4. This quatrain was rearranged significantly to allow for sensible translation.

27 This the great emperor deemed worthy
To be the opponent of himself;
And his crown of glory, to be woven of victory
Over Zrínyi and Szigetvár, to bring to fruition.

28 Let no one then, lords, by daring
Be seized, or ill-conceived nobility,
For Zrínyi Croat bán is such a foe,
Against whom a mad rush will be harmful."

29 Thus ended his words Sokolovich Mehmet.
Rushtan, the emperor's son-in-law, began his speech;
He did sit in the first place beside the great *kajmekan.*[5]
With dignity, he turns his eyes on all:

30 "Here, where the flowers of the world are gathered,
Many brave-hearted lords, all having taken part in battle;
Where the grand emperor himself is present,
Powerless is my mind in such a great council.

31 Who conquered the world with considered might,
Is in no need of such advice as a general such as I can
give,
But as he commands, what I achieve with my mind,
I do not hide, with my pure and capable heart.

32 For we are in such a place, where such secrecy
To us and to our emperor could be detrimental;
Our first sin could be followed by grave harm—
May prophecy be far from my words.

33 Here is that Zrínyi, whose great fame
Even across the sea has reached our ears,

5. A Turkish representative; in this case, Sokolovich Mehmet.

Whether his valor is true or false,
I do not know, but this is enough: amongst nations he has fame.

34 Skirmishes are fought with fame;
Not, as we think, are words small matters;
From these are wrecked mighty camps,
With these are defeated, are victorious, world emperors.

35 We, however, thinking nothing of these,
Without fortifications, foolhardily attacked Sziget;
In broad daylight we brought forces under it,
Without guards, or hidden spies.

36 Dearly have we paid for our foolhardiness,
For on this field we shed our blood;
Even now everywhere we see our fallen,
We see the Almás's waters churning corpses.

37 Who would not wonder at our unadvised affair,
How have we been cocksure of ourselves,
Could we not mock Ali Kurt's trial:
Daring to bring two thousand scimitars under Sziget?

38 Was it not Osman basha's responsibility,
That with ten thousand cavalry he would charge the castle;
They sent him to prowl on the meadows,
And supplies to Sziget to intercept.

39 Foolish daring, see where it brought him,
Under Fort Sziget he encamped his troops,
Without a bridge he released his forces into the Almás,
The greater part of his forces he shamefully lost.

40 Many with Osman basha went ahead stealthily,
He thought, into Sziget they will swiftly charge;

Murtazan basha's fine son was lost,
Deli Vid's lance killed Hamvivan.

41 We need not gamble with those fallen in desperation,
And battle with them we must avoid,
For, like vicious demons, they are ready to destroy,
From no power are these afraid.

42 Now, this is all done, let us take lesson from our injury,
Let us not await our feet's second stumbling:
At our camp's outskirts, let us post sentries,
For indeed, asleep we will come to harm.

43 As for that which concerns the taking of the fort,
With trenches we must circle it roundabout;
Thus infidels will not be able to come out upon us,
In not many days, unharmed, we will celebrate inside.

44 With cannons let us destroy the bastions filled with
earth,
With excavations let us dry out water-filled moats;
Shovels and ammunition take forts,
Sitting, we can watch the infidels, unto their doom."

45 After these words Rushtan beg sits in his place,
From elsewhere Tatar Deliman rises to his feet.
This one's wrathful heart is full of rage,
Against Rushtan he in turn bravely began to speak:

46 "I would wish, lords, that ten lands myself
Would separate from here; that I would not see
And now not hear this, our shame,
Which, trying to be wise, this one spoke.

47 Not with such council conquered the world
Noble Muslim blood; not with such is forced to give tribute

Infidels to the Turks; the sun has not heard such.
Says he: sitting, let us take the fortress.

48 It will be best: let us hide, throw away our swords,
Let us let our fame rot, let us take spades
Into our warrior hands: thus destroys infidels
The invincible emperor, thus takes castles.

49 Warriors are armed with fame,
Therefore spades win Turks fame.
Not to foxes, badgers is Sziget home,
Who may at any time be gouged out with peasant shovels.

50 Let him hide himself, he who is afraid of arms;
Let him throw aside his scimitar, he who runs like the wind;
But these our hearts, which trust in weapons,
The bright noon will not see us tilling the ground.

51 Osman stupidly lost his division;
Are we therefore shamed by it?
Yesterday backs were quickly turned on wisdom,
Are all in this army of like mind, then?

52 Allow me to say this, bluntly:
Who freed yesterday Rushtan in yesterday's battle
From Zrínyi's sword? I do not attribute it
To my courage, nor do I credit it to that.

53 Cunning Zrínyi took note of him whom before he must
flee,
He was ready to pursue Rushtan to the very camp;
Deliman he did not wish to come into close quarters with.
We all saw this: he too can flee.

54 Not shovel, not spade is our victory,
But our terrible leaden weapons;

With these Szigetvár we will quickly reduce to dust.
With these will grow our name and fame.

55 Ask not, how I will enter Szigetvár,
If Zrínyi comes out, also will I in his footsteps
Go in Szigetvár's great gates;
Let him bring spade, shovel, who puts his trust in them."

56 At such words Rushtan's heart was saddened,
Again he rose to his feet beside the *kajmekan,*
But the knight Deliman in great rage departed,
He did not condescend to hear Rushtan's words.

57 Demirham's place in the council's proceedings was still
far off,
But furiously he also arose with a shout:
"I too did not come to garden under this castle;
If that is needed, I will bring a thousand asaps.

58 Indeed it is useful council, to sit here, lounging,
For him who wishes to lose his nobility:
Likewise, thus must he act.
Do we want ourselves laughed at?

59 Deliman's good council I too advise,
And further this humiliation will not listen to.
Whoever appreciates his own good name will follow me,
I know."
With such words Demirham went out the tent door.

60 Rushtan in his anger is all but eating his hands, feet,
That these mock his wise advice,
"O, foolish nation!" he pleadingly cries,
"Not men, but stupid and enraged animals!

61 Go, take Sziget with your valiant swords,
Knock down its towers with your angry throats!
Now I see, the Turks' fate is lost,
When its council swells with madmen.

62 But what do I care about others' stupidity?
It will be better for me to sit 'til death at my tent's door,
And to wonder at the courage of these;
If indeed our endeavor must fail, then so let it fail."

63 Rushtan from the tent angrily steps out;
Petraf, who took Gyula, rises
To his feet, and thus speaks to the Turkish generals,
They who, awaiting Petraf, all watch:

64 "This angry spirit that I see amongst you,
In the middle of Szigetvár I desire,
You know, Lord God, that to you I beseech
Most of all for this cause, and frequently cry.

65 Unity makes small things great,
Weakened morale it raises high,
But the great and powerful are beaten to the ground,
If disunity touches them.

66 How many great kingdoms because of just this were lost!
It hurt the Assyrians, Greeks,
Even the Romans and other Christians,
Those who because of this were, to a man, lost.

67 This our kingdom is so great and strong that
No outside power can threaten it,
But its sheer size will not be enough for it,
If evil divisiveness worms its way into its midst.

68 Just one example I bring now before you
Which not long ago your eyes beheld;
But you from it may take much to heart,
And divisiveness between us you may recognize as harm.

69 Kalender Chelebi, Chash Bektash's nation,
Once Anatolia he had shaken up,
With ten thousand dervishes[6] he terrified
The whole of Asia, and astoundingly wrecked them.

70 What harm could sanjays'[7] strength do him?
His growing force beat those;
And that Ibrahim basha defeated him
Was the cause of his unexpected death.

71 A very small reason it was, for which Kalender this fate
Received: among the Turks a harmful storm created
Karamani[8]
With his divisiveness, and so by him everything was lost.

72 So now we, who stare into our enemies' eyes:
All of our fate rests on his courage.
What can we hope for, if such disunity
Will exist in our council, and in this army?

73 For the sake of the living God, put aside for now
Everyone from their own hearts divisiveness!
Let everyone bring this to mind confidently:
Our emperor, our honor is here with us, now.

6. Actually, the name for adherents of the mystical Sufi sect; often used to mean any Muslim warriors.

7. A class of Ottoman infantry.

8. This line is deliberately truncated by the author.

74 That, however, which has to do with the taking of Sziget,
Everyone may recognize in his heart,
That if our camp is not fortified,
Easily, the Turkish emperor could lose it.

75 For indeed, a man builds a house against wolves;
On the meadow a shepherd builds a lean-to against the rain;
Why would a trench here be shameful for us,
Some protection against our enemies?

76 Thus far we have always had to fight Zrínyi
Whenever he was in a mood to;
Often ten-twenty people made a great racket,
One drumbeat the entire camp put on edge.

77 I do not say that we should not go to battle,
Or that we should uselessly lie about here;
Indeed, a great portion of our fame we have lost,
To win it back, on that we must plot.

78 If Zrínyi bán comes out sometime to do battle,
Let us not remain then in this trench,
But not foolishly, for then it will be to our detriment,
But in ordered ranks let us charge them.

79 This is my opinion, but if someone knows better,
Let him say it, not incur my wrath by it;
And gladly I hear another man's council."
Here Petraf, having ended, sits down and grows quiet.

80 All leave Petraf's council standing,
Good and useful they all acclaim this;
Then, bowing heads in order to the *kajmekan,*
From the tent to their own dwellings disperse.

81 The Tatar Deliman went in to the emperor,
Because he long had asked for audience, and to him spoke thus:
"Powerful commander of the valiant Turks,
Hear the reason for which I have come before you!

82 At your council, I saw a wondrous thing:
There are many who desire idleness more,
Rather than to bravely draw sword against enemies,
For at home they have grown accustomed to leisurely lordship.

83 My lord, take hold of yourself in time,
Do not accept everyone's cowardly advice,
Verily, few take notice of their own shame,
Just so that they may extend their length of life.

84 I take note of the enemy's doings:
If they lose from amongst themselves their six captains,
And Zrínyi, Croat bán, he who controls all,
They will all fall, and will lose the fort.

85 Give permission for six strong knights from among us
To call Zrínyi and the other five to a duel to the death.
I swear to God, into your hand we will give
Zrínyi, and Szigetvár we will immediately conquer.

86 If, however, those do not fall from among them,
Truly much sorrow they will give us,
For greatly famed is their strength,
From which every man in your army is terrified.

87 I, I, if my previously valiant hand
Has not changed (and it has not), take this upon myself,

I will take off that thief's head,
And under your powerful foot I will place it.

88 In your army others can be found, too,
Who by such efforts are not sickened;
I believe that the noble Demirham will not hide,
Nor will Idriz Zagatar of this be terrified."

89 At the youthful Tatar's valiant heart the emperor
Greatly delights, but his mind
No such thing can cross: he does not believe in his heart,
That Zrínyi would come out of Sziget into such danger.

90 Says he to Deliman: "O, you flower of nobility!
You can worthily be admired by the entire Turkish world;
Your courageous heart is joy to me,
Do not desire, that it should be removed from me so soon.

91 Not for such a thing was born your noble arm
That in ruled combat you should throw it away,
The Muslim faith requires greater things from you:
Save your useful life for greater things.

92 Look at combat's constantly turning tide,
Not for long can it stand in one place.
What would say this world, if you to death
I would expose, and to such grave danger?

93 Have mercy on your august father, whose only son you are,
With your fate do not bring him death,
You are the strong staff of his old age,
Do not break away from him in his infirmity."

94 But Deliman does not accept the emperor's council,
But from good medicine he grows sick, and cries:

"You who diligently hold concern for me,
Let it go, and allow me for glory to suffer death.

95 We, too, in our powerful grips carry iron,
And from our wounds, too, spills red blood, we know,
Far away will be his Szigetvár, we'll see,
Into which he can hide, if our irons are there."

96 Suleiman indeed sees Deliman's fury,
And his will bent on danger,
Speaks thus: "I will not defy your will,
Let it be, as you yourself will.

97 But a better opportunity is required for this;
Now, however, differently Zrínyi's strength
We must try; Sziget with cannons
We must assault; it is now the time for that.

98 If with those we cannot hurt Sziget,
Then we will have need for your noble hand.
All of us they would mock now,
If thus our warriors we would needlessly throw away.

99 My son, I love you, I love your glory,
Remove, then, from me all your doubt;
I know well the timing of this thing,
Entrust to me just one part of your valiant heart."

PART NINE

1 Where have I wound up with my light pen?
But I could have learned from Daedalus's[1] son—
With too little preparation, I set out across the ocean;
It is a small mind, which writes about my Father's affairs.

2 History and poetry desire peace,
Not with angry Mars lives the Muses' son;
Resounding drum, trumpet do not call forth Apollo
From poetry to war and skirmishes.

3 Me, however, as I write these,
Mars' war drum and trumpet stir up.
Now bring into my house a smoking ember
The Kanjinzan Turks;[2] I must put it out.

4 Even so, not unadvisedly have I begun my work,
Knowing how much I owe to this history;
I do not hide my talent taken from God:
With arms, too, if possible, I follow my Father.

5 Tirelessly, Ali Kurt is whirling,
In three places great earthworks are built by him,
From whence by artillery Szigetvár is being shelled,
By day and by night too its walls are crumbling.

1. In Greek mythology, Daedalus fabricated wings from wax and feathers to enable himself and his son, Icarus, to escape from captivity in a tower. Despite his father's warning, Icarus flew too close to the sun, his wings melted, and he fell to his death in the sea below.

2. This particular section of the Turkish forces entered the author's domain in 1648.

6 Two days have already passed, Zrínyi from Szigetvár
Is not going out to war, for very great reason,
Though ceaselessly by the knight Deli Vid
He is asked, to be released from Szigetvár.

7 But Zrínyi to Deli Vid spoke thus:
"He who does not bridle Fortune
But gives freedom to her boastful mouth,
Will seize her in the end, only to his own demise.

8 Up until now fortune has been faithful to us,
God through His mercy has given victory;
But as it is fickle, if it begins to turn its back,
Once and for all it will drown us in danger and
deadly foam.

9 Believe, not for nothing have I been resting in here,
Great things I contemplate in my wise heart.
If the Turks were to become overconfident in this place,
I would that they believe that we are afraid.

10 Then unexpectedly we would charge them,
Destruction and chaos we would greatly inflict upon them,
In that time, perhaps to the emperor[3] we could send word,
And perhaps from him more quickly receive help.

11 Greatly did Vid affirm his lord's council,
And right there he immediately offered up himself:
"If it be your wish, my lord, my efforts
From you I do not hold back, nor the spilling of my blood.

12 Either by day or by night if you command, I will set out,
I will go amongst the Turks, because I know their tongue,

3. I.e., Emperor Maximilian.

If by craft I do not accomplish anything,
With my strength, my sword I will go through them."

13 "My dear noble servant" (thus answered Zrínyi)
"There is no need to doubt in your courage,
But you Sziget must not leave,
Here with me you must protect it.

14 Perhaps God has ordered someone else to do this thing,
Who with less loss can shoulder this responsibility."
Zrínyi with Deli Vid spoke thus,
And meanwhile ceaselessly sounded Ali Kurt's artillery.

15 Radivoj's turn for sentry duty
It was, and beside him, for Juranics vajda.
These were standing watch above the gate;
Radivoj spoke thus to his friend:

16 "Juranics vajda, my dear noble friend,
See what I have thought up, my dear right hand![4]
He, our good lord, I see in grave concern,
How to give the Magyar king word of the Turks.

17 Everywhere I know well the land,
By night I could execute such a plan.
Until it arises, I will await the splendid moon;
But first I will tell the lord this plan.

18 Believe, what great daring has entered my heart,
The like of which I've never known in my life,
It seems to me, even by day in the Turkish army
By my hand I could accomplish a great thing."

4. Literally, "right wing."

19 When vajda Radivoj spoke such things,
They ignited the other vajda's heart,
Therefore from Juranics there was such reply:
"Where then, Radivoj, would you leave me?

20 Alone upon such danger yourself
You would fling, and leave here your friend,
He who loves you, even as himself?
You flee then, Radivoj, from myself and my heart?

21 I did not conduct myself today in such a way
That of myself I could have left doubt in your heart:
In Demirham's sight, I killed a flagbearer;
Together with his life, his flag I took.

22 Though this was not my first trial,
Together with you I have done greater things.
My life for my death I too will trade,
When coupled to it is my eternal glory."

23 Radivoj, at this, thus: "God preserve you thus,
My dear noble friend, with good fortune,
Never of you in my wise mind
Did I think such cowardice.

24 But in my thoughts this is whirling:
If (as she has grown accustomed to) fortune with me
Practices evil against my wishes,
And gives me into Turkish hands dead, or alive,

25 For that, valiant companion, I desire your life,
So that there may be one, to bury my dead body,
Or on ransom to redeem my enslaved life;
You are younger, worthily extend your life."

26 Juranics does not bow under such speech;
Rather he grows furious at such placation,
And grows his desire for greater danger;
Such gilded words come upon his tongue:

27 "You futilely soothe me,
Never will you soften my heart;
May fortune heap all dangers
On my young head, but I go with you."

28 So go the two vajdas before Zrínyi,
There where he is with Deli Vid in deep discussion.
Calls forth Radivoj: "Do not wonder in your heart
My lord, that we two have come before you.

29 We saw from the towers the great stupidity
Of our enemies, and their idleness;
Yesterday with much drink they burdened their heads,
Now confidently they sleep, not knowing us.

30 If you allow, we will go now, with fortune;
We two will pass through the camp confidently,
We will take word to the emperor, who is in Vienna now,
What an enemy has encircled Sziget now.

31 Around here I know well all the earth's secrets,
Ceaseless hunting has taught me that;
Stealthily, we will steal through the Turkish camp:
Let God give fortune; he, who can give all."

32 Here in his joy Zrínyi sheds a tear,
Embracing them he shouts into the heavens:
"O, almighty God, you who defeat armies,
Not enough can my tongue bless you.

33 You do not yet wish to destroy us completely,
As you give among us such brave hearts.
But what will be reward for you enough,
O knights, worthy of all praise?

34 Hear, Sirs Radivoj and Juranics,
That which I now swear to you before God:
If this you execute successfully,
And I may be freed from my enemies,

35 All of you will be partakers in my treasure.
A rich Turkish sword, Radivoj, will be
Yours, which I from Mehmet basha won,
And a like bit for your horse, also.

36 To Juranics I give a beautiful gold helmet,
Which Gyafer along with his life left
On the beautiful meadows of Varasd, where his father fled,
To each along with these, six hundred gold, apiece."

37 So give answer the two noble vajdas:
"O, powerful warrior, Sziget's great lord,
We respect your offer, but put it elsewhere,
Gifts do not compel us to trials.

38 But glory gives us courage for this,
Which envious time cannot take from us,
Only let your head remain in good health,
We will always find these with you."

39 When Zrínyi released the knights,
Deli Vid through the doorway accompanied them,
To each he gave a fine memento,
With that he rewarded the knights:

40 Taking from himself, gave to Radivoj
Skin of the great Arab lion,
Which he took from the body of Abdus Elam,
Along with the life of Singer bég's son.

41 A fine gold-woven shirt of crimson satin
Afterward Deli Vid takes off of himself;
This he pulled off of Saracen Hamvivan,
To Juranics vajda he gives it as a gift.

42 "I hope you will wear this fortuitously."
So says Deli Vid; but the other knights
Some swords, some helmets give them;
Armed, then, toward the gate they go.

43 It was in the hour when all creatures
Most peacefully unto themselves rest
Take; shepherd, plowman sleep their sweet dreams,
By the sheep sleeps the sheepdog, who has tired.

44 Then the knights go out both,
They call Jehovah into their hearts for help,
They have bravery and great hope,
Toward everywhere they are on guard in the darkness.

45 They do not go from the fortress to a very far land,
They see many Turks on the ground sprawled,
They think: which way would it be best to go,
Where most likely the Turks could not notice them?

46 Verily, two wild wolves are these similar to,
When every which way they watch livestock;
All of them they would gladly attack,
Finally from where the most cry out, they charge.

47 Radivoj to Juranics says in whisper:
"Our path guard, my dear noble companion.
I ahead will make way with great strength,
Because Turks lie here, drunk."

48 After such words greedy Perviz's neck
From his body he cut; this one upon the Magyar soldiers
Looked on as nothing, believing himself greater
Than thirteen Christians' might.

49 Afterwards Rézmán's chest he cleaves in two,
He gushes much blood mingled with wine,
Here strong Begzade loses his life:
The scimitar consumes Kaitas and Rechep.

50 Wherever go the two vajdas with arms,
They paint tent and earth aplenty with Turkish blood;
Many nameless people fall by the sword,
Because of two courageous hands, all across the field.

51 Two camps they have already cut their way through,
Still do not notice the horrific destruction
The intoxicated Turks; from wine is blinded
Even the one who is wise: good he cannot tell from bad.

52 Into the third camp, where Suleiman is lying,
The two noble lions furiously arrive:
The tiny tents they all avoid,
They come into the one where Kadilesker is lying.

53 What use to you was piety, Kadilesker?
Your future-telling worthlessly does not remain;
Amfiaraus also was so wise a man,
But was once disappointed by his intelligence.

54 Juranics with sword creeps slowly to his bed,
With both hands reaches for his sharp scimitar,
Raising it slashes to his exposed neck,
His head rolls down to the fine green felt.

55 Somehow his page noticed this,
Shouts; but not long was his cry,
Radivoj's blow sends after his lord
His unlucky soul under the deep earth.

56 Beside Kadelisker on a gilded couch
Lies on a velvet pillow the Turkish Al-Koran.
This memento Juranics, for having passed such trial,
Took with him, Radivoj spoke thus:

57 "Accomplished, Juranics, are all our plans,
A path for ourselves among the Turks we have made,
But it is not good for us to toy further with fortune,
Let us come out from among them; 'tis not good to enjoy ourselves here."

58 For long they dodge the many tents,
Finally they leave, there where the border was
Of that great camp; the Almás river's bank
On the right they leave behind, and do not follow the road.

59 Not far from the camp three thousand Tatars
Walk the sentry duty, and there Zagatar Idriz
Is present himself; he walks round and round,
That from the infidels no evil may befall from behind.

60 These notice the two noble vajdas,
The forerunner shouts "Kimszi? Kimszi?"[5]

5. Turkish: "Who are you? Who are you?"

Now no hope can either one see,
Both flee toward the forest, as quickly as they can.

61 Now Radivoj does not fear, for he has gone into the forest,
But the other was not possessed of such speed;
This one the Tatars surrounded all around,
So that he was not left with any hope.

62 Radivoj looks back, and does not see his friend;
Think of his terrible sorrow.
"Juranics! Juranics!" he cries through the thick forest,
But none other than Echo gives him sad reply.

63 "Juranics! Juranics! where have I left you?
To what dogs as prey have I given you?
Where shall I look for you now, and where shall I find
    you?
On the ground of what earth shall I track you down?"

64 Thus he weeps and thus he shouts, and retraces his path,
That somehow Juranics's trail he might recognize.
Great shouts he hears; there he returns,
Sees Juranics, that among Turks he is.

65 What shall he do himself, and with what weapon
Can he bring out his beloved friend from among the
    Turks?
If he charges them by himself, it helps not
His friend at all, if he dies there.

66 A fine gilded handbow is at his side,
Which that night he won from the Turks,
This he quickly snatches along with arrows from the quiver,
The arrow he pulls back to his ear.

67 Flies the feathered arrow; into Shabasot's chest
It lodges, and runs him through;
He falls dead into his friend's lap,
But his friend another arrow strikes in the left ear.

68 There about Juranics eight dead Tatars lie,
Who has caused this, no one knows,
However Captain Idriz arrives there,
In front of his eyes two Tatars fall.

69 Grieves the captain, he does not see, who has made
Among his many warriors so quickly such death;
Thus he says to Juranics, drawing his scimitar:
"You will for all of them pay one death."

70 No longer can Radivoj contain his sorrow,
He clambers over to where he sees his friend,
"Me, me, soldiers!" from afar he cries,
"Kill me, not my friend!

71 I was the cause of those deaths;
I, the greater mind in this trial.
This one did nothing, but no harm can cause
Children such as this to such a powerful army."

72 But the cruel Tatar his entreaty
Lets pass by his ear, and his scimitar in the head
Of Juranics he sinks; he falls there prone,
And releases his soul's purity mingled with blood.

73 Falls Juranics, like a tender flower
Who a callous worker with a great sickle mows down,
Or if a lily falls by its roots,
Which stood in a spring meadow, in fine growth.

74 Like a wild leopard, if it loses its cub,
And if it finds before itself the hunters' party,
Upon them its fury, teeth; upon them it brings to bear its claws,
Spears it crushes in heaps, but there loses its life:

75 Thus enraged Radivoj charged upon the foe;
Amongst the great forces, he keeps Idriz in sight;
Many hundreds of blows he took upon himself,
He does not think, because for his friend he will take vengeance.

76 Idriz among the soldiers he has now found,
With one blow at the waist he cleaves him in two,
He himself from wounds falls prone,
Beside his companion he commends his soul to God.

77 O, blessed; O, happy; O, noble knights!
If my Magyar verses can do anything about it,
Never will your admirable fame
Die, as long as flow the rapid waters.

78 Until the sun stops, as long as the Magyar nation
With sword protects the Christian faith,
Your names will live; you, however, the Lord
In eternal bliss now praise.

79 Meanwhile Deli Vid in the outer palace
Falls into a deep sleep before the Lord's house;
Just like that, armed, in helmet and mail,
Sitting in a wide window, he sleeps.

80 Suddenly he jumps up, like one who has lost his mind,
He went to his lord, and began to speak thus:

"My lord, all hope has fallen from my heart;
The two vajdas have just now died."

81 Amazed, the good Zrínyi hears this,
And in answer, he wisely says this:
"Why do you allow your hard heart to weep
Like a little girl? Hold back your tears,

82 They do not suit you: you shriek like a premature-born.
Ill Fate must not befall a soldier unprepared;
Evil we must await, ready in our hearts,
But not just occasionally, but at all times.

83 Now I ask you this: where did you hear
Of the two strong vajdas' deaths?"
But Deli Vid cannot restrain his weeping,
Replies to his lord such wise words:

84 "Do not wonder at my heart, that it weeps bitterly,
For it was badly pierced by that cruel news.
A man cannot always bear his heart,
If he loses that which was promised him by fate.

85 That the thoughts of my soul I may soften,
First I sat down on a comfortable chair;
I had hardly closed my tired eyes,
When Sir Radivoj came before me.

86 Truly, I saw him so armed,
As when from myself I had dismissed him,
But covered in many scars and grave wounds;
I could barely recognize who it was.

87 In a hundred places was opened his noble breast,
And so many wounds more carried his noble head.

Helmet, lion hide, which covered him,
With much dried blood were infected.

88 Ah, so different was that from the Radivoj
Who in Sziget had brought Abdullah along with his son
Bound, who had brought many weapons as prey,
Which he had won by his own hand from the Turks!

89 That I spoke to him, it seemed to me:
'Who dealt thus with you, o you noble vajda?
This dried blood which disfigures your body,
Who, by arms, caused you to spill it?

90 Not thus awaited you Sziget's captain,
He who is in great concern for you;
Sziget's host is in great hope also,
Your courage was to be its aid.'

91 He, however, to these did not reply
At all, only looks at me with sad eyes;
After much sighing finally in Croatian tongue
Says this to me with bitterness:

92 'As long as God willed it, Deli Vid, I lived,
But for the Christian faith I have now suffered death
Together with Juranics, and now have come before you,
I, naked spirit; with the Turks is my body.

93 Nothing recoil, Deli Vid, from me;
In not much time you will be with me,
For martyrdom to you also God
Has allotted, your lord and all, and a place in the heavens.

94 Do not forget then your courage,
And do not be terrified of the pagan Turks,

I beg strength for you from God;
God be with you, stand bravely.'

95 Thus he spoke, and disappeared, as a quick breeze before me,
As a light shadow in the air;
Vainly I ran after him, that I may embrace him
Thrice, but my hands fell only on nothingness."

96 Hardly could Vid finish his sad words,
Than from the bastions they heard a hellish racket.
In the Turkish camp a great clamor had arisen,
For only now had they realized their great losses.

97 Here the dead commander the Tatars bring,
Their bright flags they turned to the ground,
With terrible noise they bewail their lord,
His arms and best horse they bring behind his corpse.

98 Elsewhere for Kadilesker a burial is being prepared,
Nearly the entire camp gathers to that spot.
There stands Mihaliogli, there the many generals around,
They wonder, that such a thing came about from two knights.

99 Suleiman mourns the great Kadilesker,
For he had never met one wiser than he.
But to come forth from his tent the emperor did not even dare;
So upon him no one noticed a change.

100 Both to one place the generals had brought,
Afterwards stripped them of everything.
With Arabian balsam embalmed them,
Into a shallow space placed both of them.

101 Over the funerals wailed the hodjas;[6]
Not to despair, they encourage the Turks.
Many dervishes and talismans[7] call forth Mahomet
To them for aid, and afterward leave them.

6. Meuzzins who call the faithful to their daily prayers.
7. Turkish clerics.

PART TEN

1 Wandering and cruel fortune on the same path
Across every age is not content to stay, and the same;
For sometimes she dresses in a joyful face,
And sometimes runs in full fury.

2 She rejoices in nothing as she does in change,
Because in nighttime and daytime and at every hour
She changes, and is in constant motion;
But most of all, in time of war.

3 So far with favor she had showed herself to Sziget,
She had conducted herself against her own nature
For long, but now changed her stride,
Tore from her neck her heavy leash.

4 Everything that she could, danger and battle,
Afterward she spewed on Sziget, and terrible sorrow;
At her early generosity she was now angered,
She now became a wide-mouthed venom well.

5 Fortune likes to toy with brave hearts,
But the brave do not tend to give in to her.
However a pilot against powerful undertow
May struggle, so must a brave heart struggle with her.[1]

6 Shrinks and softens the heart of the timid
In evil luck, but not Zrínyi's;

1. This stanza has been rearranged significantly for ease of translation.

In fact, his courage grows, if danger
He sees increasing, and ill fortune.

7 He sees that Sziget's town has burned,
One of the castle's towers has collapsed from the artillery,
Readying for siege already are many janissaries and gyumlias,[2]
Many hundreds of thousands of people he sees, coming to his danger.

8 Like howling demons, the time of the siege
Await the brave Turks, the signal for battle;
They crave, thirst for good Zrínyi's blood,
And together with his blood, that of the rest of the Christians.

9 The outer and inner town were now with the Turks,
Which Zrínyi himself wisely abandoned,
For all his strength into the fortress he had brought;
That he wishes to keep until his own head falls.

10 Sounded then many drums and trumpets,
Many mingled peoples they readied to war;
Many horsemen were encouraged by brave hearts,
Leaving behind their good horses, infantry ran to do battle.

11 Onto the collapsed tower ran brave Demirham,
After him six thousand janissaries and spahoglans,[3]
Charges at the gate strong and great-hearted Deliman,
After him eight thousand Tatars and Muslims.

12 Three thousand Albanians, two thousand Carmanians,
Three thousand Cirkanians after Aigas basha,

2. Volunteer cavalrymen.
3. Regular cavalry.

Carry from a third direction picks on their backs,
There is Singir zagatar, Saracen Kenan.

13 In the fortress's central square, however, stood
Zrínyi bán, in his hand is a gilded lance,
Behind him the host stood in a group,
Listening to its lord's fine encouraging words.

14 On Henyei's bastion, that which was ruined,
Radován Andrián stood with a hundred infantrymen.
With a hundred swords guarded the gate Péter Bot;
Everyone was in their allotted place:

15 There where Aigas basha readied his ladders
Deli Vid with a hundred swords guards the bastion,
Novákovics Iván beside him the other one,
Everyone, ready, awaits the enemy's sword.

16 Now, out of the trenches pour the many countless Turks—
Not this many came out of the Trojan horse's side;
Some picks, some axes, some carry scimitars on their sides,
Some the sudden death, firearms, carry on their backs.

17 The moat's ditch is knee-high for the Turks,
Because the rest of the water they earlier released,
But on this straw and branches they still poured,
So that they could go to siege with greater ease.

18 In front, Demirham carries a spear in his hand,
A shield in the other, a falcon-feather on his head,
A breastplate on his chest, and he comes in front,
The soldier brings death, brings danger into Sziget.

19 Bravely he charged at the castle's moat,
Thinks nothing of that his companions are falling;

Beside him and above him shots fly,
Many lodge in the iron in the center of his chest.

20 He with hands, he with eyes, he with his brave advance
Reassures his companions with his ferocious throat,
When he reaches there where the opened wall
Shows Radován with a hundred noble scimitars.

21 Like the enraged dragon that sees close its prey
Readies its venomous claws and blood-gorged throat,
With fury sharpens its hooked fangs,
Swims in venom, with venom swells:

22 Thus Demirham strides and cruelly silent,
His fury does not elicit sound from his throat,
He only rages within himself, and holds his heavy spear;
He runs through Poki's massive side.

23 Falls Poki Gergely, and copiously spills his blood,
With his blood he releases from himself his spirit,
But immediately finds there his burial,
For two hundred dead Turks covered his corpse.

24 For Radován by his own hand twice twenty
Fells in a heap above him, brave janissaries.
Medvei Benedek Testoglin and Operka
Kills above him, and ten more Muslims.

25 Orostoni Péter cuts down Saladin,
But Demirham kills him, strong Orostoni;
Malkuch Huszár, Szelim Balázs, and Gerdei,
But Bosnyák kills Benavir, Ramadan, Husain.

26 Achmedani aga set himself on this,
That he would charge Radován, and to him shouts thus:

"Do you recognize, infidel, the powerful Achmedan,
He who will cause you to drop below the ground?"

27 With both hands he strikes at him, crying thus,
But the other one takes up the blow on his shield;
Thus the noble vajda replies to him immediately:
"And I am the Croat vajda Radován."

28 He says no more, but strikes at him mercilessly,
The other falls dead to the ground before him,
His spirit, leaving his body, flies below the ground,
Of blood and warmth his body once and for all cools.

29 Demirham himself does the most:
By his hand Haszanovics falls there,
Afterward Penezics by him is killed,
Hajdu Mátyás, Nagy Máté before him lie.

30 But before Radován wallow in blood
Pirim, Baluk basha, and ten other wounded Turks.
Now are confounded together in this place
Turks and Christians, in the great chaos.

31 Some half-dead but still alive cry for their companions,
Some on the horribly hard ground whimper;
Between blood and arms sound the wretched appeals,
You would think from afar, that the sky has fallen.

32 Lies among the dead, though still alive,
Sir Szlamenovics (for his leg at his knee
Was broken, the unfortunate); he cries to the sky,
The ruinous gun in the Turk's hands he curses.

33 But when approaches him Terhat aga,
From the ground the Turk's clothing he catches,

With his other hand into his chest he thrusts his lance,
He pulls the Turk down beside him, dead.

34 He strikes at Demirham too with expended strength;
Foolish, he does not know that greater power
Is needed to kill this one; Demirham with his weapon
Takes up the blow, and with great speed

35 Separates his head from his body right there.
But here arrives then also great Radován;
As over prey two sinewy lions
Collide, carrying fire in their hearts:

36 So the two warriors come together with daring.
First Demirham strikes at him with his scimitar,
But the vajda takes it up with his shield,
Likewise strikes immediately with his great sword.

37 Strikes at him, but the sword shatters in his grip
(Traitor, leaving its master in time of danger);
As he bitterly looks at his unarmed hand,
Demirham cuts his helmet in two.

38 Even so, the noble vajda does not frighten,
Though his head from the blow was stunned,
Covering himself with shield he runs under the sword,
Grasping his furious opponent's flank.

39 Gladly would Demirham separate from his opponent,
For now cramped, he cannot reach him with his sword,
But the other does not release him from himself,
So the two began to wrestle in anger.

40 Here and there they throw themselves,
From tripping, from falling, they guard well their feet.

The Saracen crushes to himself the vajda,
And the vajda the Saracen, as well as he can.

41 When honey-scent falls into the bear's nose,
Climbing after it, it falls from the beech tree;
With claw and tooth it attacks the tree,
Shreds uselessly its bark to its roots:

42 Thus both of them circle the other,
Each eagerly awaits harm upon the other's head,
Demirham is enraged, like a flood swollen from snow,
But the other, as long as he lives, wants to give him no quarter.

43 The last thread of great Radován's life
Are spinning the merciless Parcae,[4]
For as soon as Durak came behind him,
Into the vajda he rammed half his spear.

44 Onto the black ground toppled the poor vajda,
But even so he drags fortune with him,
Half-dead on the ground he still maims his enemy,
Until the unfortunate was abandoned by his soul entirely.

45 Trembled the hard ground under the two warriors.
Have you seen fall an ancient oak tree,
Which a creeping ivy felled with great ropes?
Thus lies Radován under the pagan, dead.

46 Terrible Demirham rises from the ground,
Charges at more enemies, like a whirlwind;

4. The Fates of Roman and Greek mythology; three sisters who spun and cut the threads that indicated the passage of men's lives. The first half of this quatrain was rearranged significantly for ease of understanding.

No one dares await his attack, for they are afraid,
For in his hand is cruel death, great danger.

47 The vajda-less knights abandoned the bastion,
Run to and fro, like little children;
But here comes Dandó, brings worry to the Turks,
With a hundred noble blades aids the fleeing army.

48 Inadequate, Dandó, is your help:
If Zrínyi himself more reinforcements
Does not bring quickly, you will lose Sziget,
For the fallen bastion has received two thousand Turks.

49 Everything in his power Dandó does himself,
For many thousands of blows he takes upon his shield:
Countless Turks he fells in one place,
Like a giant, wallows in his enemies' blood.

50 From elsewhere Deliman arrives at the gate,
He death, he danger in his strong hand brings;
The great lance in his hand resembles an oak tree,
Or a terrible galley ship's mast.

51 More courage enters Bot Péter's heart
Than he ought to have in such times,
For he goes out to battle before the Turks,
Shrugging off the Turks, he has faith in his own heart.

52 He opens the gate of sturdy Szigetvár,
There stands before him great Deliman,
But Deliman takes the lives of a dozen,
Who diligently fight before Bot Péter.

53 Péter also from elsewhere does harm to the Turks,
For Murtuzan falls before him with a great wound,

Saban also, Bichir also, Pechlivan Eosven,
Before Sas Fabian lies Nuh Mohacen.

54 Stood Embrulah with gilded weapon,
A hat spun with golden thread is on his head,
Ornamented janissary muskets in both his hands,
Sharp Baghdadi sword dangles in its sheath.

55 He was the beloved son of Nezer Chelebi;
For his intellect was laden with all sorts of knowledge;
He was the loving servant of the Muses:
He the kobza, the miszkal, he the chingia knew.[5]

56 He with a Saracen gourd put Pan[6] to shame,
And with his song, nightingales;
To the forests he was Orpheus,[7] to the fishes Arion,[8]
Another Endimio[9] was he to the radiant moon.

57 O, eternally fortunate, Embrullah, would you be,
If battle and Sziget you could avoid!
Hither Badankovics, crueller than a bear,
Goes, brings fear by his great strength.

58 Uselessly Embrullah discharges his musket,
For it does not strike the Croat champion;

5. Various sorts of medieval instruments.

6. This is the first of several comparisons the author draws between Embrullah and figures from Greek mythology. Pan, the merry god of the forests, was an expert player of the pipes.

7. Orpheus could sing and play so beautifully that he could tame wild beasts and raise the dead.

8. Arion was one of the first poets. When captured by pirates and thrown into the sea, he sang a song so moving that he was rescued by dolphins.

9. Endymion was a prince so handsome that the goddess of the moon fell in love with him and bore his children.

He, on the other hand, seizes Embrullah from among the
masses,
Like a great albatross a delicate swan.

59 Under his arm he carries his faint, weak prey,
With his thin throat he cries for help.
Sees Deliman the young Embrullah,
He runs after Badankovich, as quickly as his feet can take
him.

60 Badankovich sees that he will not take peacefully
The Turkish youth; with the edge of his scimitar
He opens his beautiful throat, which with beautiful song
Forest, meadow filled with much wonder.

61 Stops then and waits for him who pursues him,
Deliman, lighting-quick, appears before him,
As a rapid lightning bolt, flies his great javellin.
In one blink of an eye it shreds Iván.

62 "You destroyed the world's great joy
And I, for him, have taken your life."
So Deliman speaks, and with his foot pressing his body,
From his corpse draws his spear and his blood.

63 Bot Péter regretted his intrepid attempt,
He does not dare await Deliman's fury,
He flees back to the fort, brings back his army,
Accepts the shame of his recklessness.

64 Not long afterward arrives at the gate
Deliman, resembles he the water's flood,
When rocks, fallen trees, trunks aplenty it brings,
For terror and destruction it brings in its fist.

65 Many countless Tatars fall beside him
From gunfire, of that he is not terrified;
His heart cannot fear, in fact it is nourished
By dangers, and it grows more valiant.

66 A little wooden tower was above the gate,
That wrecked now Ali Kurt by his cannon;
Tower, people and all, fall before Deliman,
Some on backs, some on feet, some on their heads fall;

67 Some are laid dead by heavy beams,
Some by their own weapons through the chest are speared,
Some the great fall led to death,
There were twenty; two aside, all were lost there.

68 Szvilojevics Antal, Klizurics Mikula,
Unharmed fell from the tower,
But when Klizurics saw himself
By many thousands of Turks surrounded,

69 Like a forest beast, falling into a bloodlust,
Should by accident a hunting party come its way,
Enraged, it charges upon the cruel weapons,
Knowing well that its death is present:

70 Klizurics also thus, where he sees thicker armaments,
Holds up his shield and draws his head under;
But in his other hand his heavy broadsword holds,
Goes hopelessly forth, seeing there his death.

71 Szvilojevics however trusts in his quick feet,
Through the Turks and through the weapons he charges in
great haste,
He grabs at the bastion, struggles with it,
To see how he could climb it, and be in safety.

72 But there the wretch is reached by cruel Deliman,
Catching him dreadfully by his foot,
He struggles up, but only uselessly,
For he yanks him down, tearing the great wall down with him.

73 "Did you believe that you could flee before me,
Faithless dog, and that you were faster than Deliman?
Thus speaks the monster to him, and with a great iron
Opens his throat, through which enters death.

74 Miklós Badankovich stands beside the gate,
And elsewhere Hervoics, like two great oaken trunks
Which on the Danube's shore here, and on the other side, stand,
Higher than the rest, and more powerful:

75 These foolishly open the gates,
That the enemy may enter, they wish aloud,
For not many they plan to allow in;
The rest held outside, the others inside they shall strike.

76 Surge the many Turks, and crawl over each other's backs,
Each one before the others wishes to enter;
But Hervoics has already grown afraid of his doing,
Closes the gate, with his shoulder bracing.

77 Foolish, for he has enclosed the Tatar king,
As among sheep an enraged lion.
Milos Badankovich stakes him out,
He charges at the brave Tatar, from afar shouts:

78 "This is not Crimea, Deliman, the land of your home,
But Sziget's fortress, and your burial;

With death you will pay for my brother,
So let this lance be thine."

79 Leaps aside Deliman, as a fleet squirrel,
Gives room to death, the lance hits the chest
Of great Daus basha, pierces his heart;
But Deliman replies thus, in reply laughs:

80 "It is more fitting that you accompany your brother's soul
To bottomless hell, and you may catch him en route."
With his great Persian sword after such words his chest
He opens, and releases his sorrowful spirit.

81 Hervoics beside him killed nine Tatars,
But he came to harm, with the loss of his life,
It did not help to enclose his life in mail,
Both were wrecked by the great Persian sword.

82 Alone remained the powerful Deliman,
For all his companions were lost in the fortress;
Still his heart is in such courage,
As if he were in the middle of the Turkish camp.

83 Neither in his words, nor on his hands, nor on his brave person
Could one recognize fear: he strides stiffly,
He treads, wades through, and mercilessly slaughters
Christian soldiers who stand before him.

84 All flee before him, avoid him like fire,
Neither did it cross his mind then
That he could have let the Turkish army into the fort,
Only upon the fleeing people did he focus his thoughts.

85 But when they heard this in the fort's central square,
That into the fortress had broken angry Deliman,

And that he was creating great destruction alone with his scimitar,
Together with Alapi Gáspár hurries vajda Stipán.

86 Then first took hold of himself
Deliman, that it is not good for him to delay in here.
As when a brave lion many armed hunters
Sees, does not flee, but furiously goes before them:

87 Deliman so strides with his sword toward the gate,
Because behind himself he sees a flood of weapons everywhere;
The crowd accompanies him with shouting, some fire at him,
Some fire, some water in rivers spew at him.

88 O, how often he turned back! He was ashamed of his flight,
He is ashamed to show the Christians his back;
He wants to go back, but his mind over his bravery
Conquers; he maintains his course toward the gate.

89 The great iron lock, which was the weight of a horse,
He smashed with his fist, kicked the gate with his foot;
Thus courageous Deliman departed from the fort,
The drawbridge was raised; he swam the moat.

90 Wise Aigas basha, with his military mind,
Brings ladders to bear on Vid with great mastery,
Many thousands of janissaries give dense fire from the shore,
On the bastion give no one room to stand.

91 But neither sleeps here smart Csontos Pál,
Plenty answers them with powder and cannon,

With tarred wreaths, flaming missiles;
He stands against the ladder-carriers, to their great harm.

92 And all their efforts, indeed, were for naught;
Aigas wonders at his own grave danger;
For there he found himself with three thousand Turks dead,
And even so, he had not been able to advance on the bastion.

93 But Demirham ruins, destroys, slaughters the crowd,
He all but destroys the Christian army alone.
Unfortunately stands before him Dandó, and hope
He has already released from his heart, for he sees few companions.

94 When Sziget's Hector saw this,
Two divisions he quickly commands;
Noble Zrínyi himself rides in front,
His weapon twinkles, the fine lance in his hand.

95 Did you tremble, Demirham, when you saw this?
Like a leaf on an aspen tree? you yourself did not deny it,
When after the battle you recounted to the emperor
The shape of the battle, and you told the truth.

96 For there was not much blood left in your face,
When you saw the bán's lance, how it strikes;
A hundred Turks with his own hand Zrínyi beats down,
Even still, he only grows in bravery.

97 Lie before him Balbozan and Bilal,
The infantryman Rez, Kurt, Ali, aga Behludi Sal;
Kassum exhales his spirit, Sulfikar bites dust,
Noble Siaus bég, Pirkuch, Porcha Alfal.

98 Like a giant in the sea, the bán wades in blood;
The many Turks writhe in their wounds;
More and still more Turks he lays out in one place;
Then begin to flee the Turk, out of ranks.

99 Who does not find an escape leaps below bastion,
Hands, feet, and the heads of some are crushed,
There are not enough Turks left on the bastion for
the siege;
Uselessly, Demirham fights alone.

100 For the great mass against his will
Yanks him suddenly out of the bastion.
Calls he aplenty: "Dur!"[10] but uselessly,
For the throng is carrying itself out from between
the walls.

101 Now many Turks are falling; like reeds before the fire,
Which the shepherd lights in the spring, and rejoices,
Seeing the hard battle of wind and fire:
So fall the many Turks, and quickly they fly.

102 You would not see other than dust and tall smoke,
Which the gentle breeze carries swirling,
Mingled with screams; danger strides among them,
Mercilessly flows the pagan Turkish blood.

103 Have you seen Death painted in a fresco,
Who horrifically carries his sickle?
The bán is so horrific in the Turkish camp,
Like grass before a sickle, so the Turks fall in heaps.

104 He gives courage to the entire host,
He gives strength to the Szigetians, and power,

10. Turkish: "Stop!"

For no one beside him has ever come to harm;
Everyone bravely wishes to be at his side in battle.

105 After long battle he returns to his fine castle,
As to her cubs the faithful she-lion,
Having dispelled danger, returns to her lair:
So does Zrínyi to his vassals return, rejoicing.

106 And they around him, like lion cubs,
Rejoice, celebrate, and praise him,
The army-defeating God they worship,
They guard, they work, and they stand ready.

PART ELEVEN

1 Even a lowly heart is spurred to greatness by revenge,
How much more the incorrigible, the one without wisdom;
Let Achilles be for this my proof,
Who was kept from battle by revenge.

2 O, if certain people could be free of this!
They could ask God for nothing better on earth,
For some vengeance passes quickly,
But some fall back on their own heads with grave harm.

3 Deliman, having returned from the terrible battle,
Tired, drenched in dried blood and dust,
But his heart even more so in vengeance,
He is ashamed that he ran from Sziget.

4 "What will Rushtan bég now say to me,
If this my shame he will hear?"
(Thus he spoke to himself), "What will think
Emperor of me, if he will know this?"

5 "O, for I have lost all my good fame!
Because I did not await my enemies before me,
They saw my back, they saw my shame,
Whereto can I now wish my life?

6 Now there will be room for my detractors,
Tongues will open to shame me,
For no-one saw my honor's
Trial, and that of my powerful arm.

7 I did not run, no, before infidel dogs,
But alone I could not repel a battle cloud;
I came out from Sziget, having left there my mark:
A lake of blood, a mountain of corpses, smoking cinders."

8 So pondered the Tatar khan's son by himself,
Meanwhile Rushtan's evil star
Led him before the youth;
Rushtan haughtily calls to Deliman thus:

9 "I thought, Crimean bég, you will bring Zrínyi bound,
As was yesterday your boast,
But perhaps deliberately you delayed that;
Perhaps you go before the emperor, to ask him for Sziget.

10 Very well, I lied, you spoke true,
The infidels with one blow you cut down,
But I regret that you fled sooner,
Rather than having wandered more slowly through Sziget."

11 Fire is not so sudden, nor gunshot,
Nor the terrible heavenly thunder,
As are massive the Tatar's heart and temper;
For immediately flashed in his hand cruel steel.

12 Uselessly Rushtan bég parries the blow with his sword,
Because with three blows the mighty Tatar khan
Lays him out dead on the ground, and above him speaks thus:
"Dead dog, this is the Crimean bég, with whom you toyed."

13 Shouting, screaming, many gather there,
For the janissary armies stood with their leader,
But Deliman thinks nothing of them;
Peacefully, he steps into his own tent.

14 Hearing such clamor the emperor himself goes to
investigate,
But arrives too late, for he sees
His dead son-in-law's affair, and asks: "For what
Reason have you received punishment from the disgraced?"

15 Kassum kapidji-basha stands before him,
Before the enraged emperor, and with spiteful words
Kindles his blazing heart, and says: "What good is it,
That you are our emperor? He dies, innocently.

16 This innocent died of our own weapons,
Which we brought upon the infidels; anathema to our faith
Is this wicked deed; but what cares for our faith
Deliman, if he fears you not, nor God?

17 For but recently in our council this lordling dared
To lecture us, and uselessly
We complained about him; now in your camp
Your son-in-law he killed in petty revenge.

18 Authority and mercy are all worthless,
If honor and fear are not the pillars;
Upon your own head I predict an evil fortune
If now Deliman goes unpunished."

19 Kassum still had more to say to the emperor,
But Demirham likewise arrived at the scene,
With a fierce gesture cut him off,
But to the emperor himself spoke thus:

20 "Invincible emperor, now remember,
Who Deliman is, for in his hands
Your camp sleeps safely.
A truly great knight, and a great lord in his land.

21 For the nation-ruling man, punishments are not uniform
Even if the crime is the same, for special judgment
Is needed in all things: sometimes the punishment
Is worse than a gentle warning."

22 The emperor responds thus: "You have advised me
wrongly,
Demirham, for there is nothing greater or better
Than justice, that which looks impartially at all;
So tell me, what good does imperium do me,

23 If only upon the wretched falls my punishment?
Do I have power only over those?
But I will show that it is not so,
For I will not allow Deliman's wrongdoing."

24 But Demirham dared not say more,
Quickly to Deliman, his friend, he went,
Of the emperor's great wrath tells him,
That because of it he should guard his life.

25 Deliman smiled as he heard this,
But into his smile mingled fire and fury.
Thus says to Demirham: "See the stupidity
Of the senile emperor; and what does he think me?

26 Perhaps I am his slave, like the other Muslims,
Or I shame my bed, like loud-mouthed Rushtan?[1]
I am not like these, Suleiman will see
To his own detriment; I am a lord, like he, and a khan.

27 Let him come himself and catch me,
Let him bring my noble head under punishment,

1. Rushtan was, apparently, impotent.

He will see how I conduct myself
Then, how I will tolerate my execution!

28 A wondrous tragedy in his mind is crafting
The emperor, which Zrínyi will mock from Szigetvár."
Saying this, he dresses quickly in only light armor,
His terrible lance takes in hand.

29 Meanwhile both Aigas and Halul have arrived;
He has always counted these as friends.
Deliman's anger they calm, and his heart;
Halul bég thus begins his speech to the Tatar:

30 "O, mighty knight, O, our pride!
Your prowess we know well,
There is nothing unreachable for you, we know well,
All before your sword are powerless, we know well.

31 But this, let God not allow us to see,
That he, behind whom we march,
By him to be destroyed, and for you against us
To draw sword, the sword from which our enemies cower.

32 Answer now, what you wish to accomplish:
Perhaps in Turkish blood your hand to defile,
Pure Mahomet's faith to render meaningless,
The infidel's pleasure to gain?

33 Ah, let it not be so, for God's sake I pray,
For there is no place here for such malice;
Strip it away from the nobility of your heart,
Submit to him, to whom all submit;

34 Retreat from the angry eyes of the emperor,
Allow a little time for his righteous anger,

This will not be cowardice; indeed, great wisdom
They will call it, whoever will hear of it.

35 We, your friends, will be here in the meantime,
And will find a way for your return,
You may live secretly in some town,
Until you hear something good from us.

36 After such counsels the heart softened
Of the young knight; immediately he began to prepare,
But he left there with only one companion
Astride his horse Duman, and said farewell to them.

37 He left peacefully, but Demirham
Cannot rest, and in fact stews within himself;
His heart is restless every hour,
Because he had met Deli Vid in battle.

38 And to him he swore, that to battle he would return,
When time gave him opportunity,
And from the Turkish emperor a written promise he would elicit,
Because of which no one else would dare hurt Deli Vid.

39 Until now his purpose had always been delayed,
For always one thing or another was in his way;
Now, however, his heart inflamed him,
And to finish the battle he truly wished from his heart.

40 Therefore he calls before him an emissary,
One who had before then undertaken many missions,
And to him thus began his speech:
"Sahman, you must execute a mission.

41 I want Sir Deli Vid to be in your sight;
Say to him: there is no forgetfulness in me;
That which I have promised, I have brought to fruition,
From the emperor a written promise I have sent him.

42 Let him be afraid of no one, come out on the field,
I myself am his only opponent,
Let him show upon me, if he has courage,
He too will see, what Demirham's hand is capable of."

43 Sahman departed for noble Sziget's fortress,
He waves from afar, that he is an emissary.
Therefore they let him in Sziget's gate.
There he inquires about Deli Vid, where he is.

44 When Sahman recognized Deli Vid,
To him he respectfully, slowly bowed his head,
There with brave tongue said to him:
"Demirham has sent me, Vid, to you.

45 If you have honor, he says to you,
Come out onto the field, there is your place,
With Demirham's arm you will become acquainted there;
For a fatal duel he comes against you.

46 No other opponent will there be for you,
Only Demirham alone will fight against you.
Deli Vid, you may believe this for all that is holy,
For here from the emperor is a written promise."

47 Like fire, Vid leapt into furious consideration,
His wrath he can no longer contain in himself,
Says he to the Turk: "Wait, but for only a moment,"
Then to the great lord he goes in the inner fortress.

48 Bowing to his feet, he begins to plead,
That he would not hesitate to send him out to battle.
Therefore reluctantly, but nothing can do the
Bán, he gives Vid leave to engage in fatal duel.

49 Vid emerges from the fortress, like a predatory eagle,
Whose beak and claws are warlike and curved;
So Deli Vid all around is gleaming metal,
His helmet on his head decorated with a terrible feather.

50 Says he to the emissary then: "Go to your lord,
Tell him what Deli Vid carries in his hand"
(A lance was in his hand); "Then await there,
Where he saw me the first day, near the stream."

51 Sahman his message delivers to his lord.
Furious thoughts flow into his[2] heart;
Much he pleads to great Allah,
Much to Mahomet, he swears to Ali.[3]

52 Fifty calves he slaughters for the poor,
That from God they may beg good fortune for him,
Much money for talismans and dervishes,
Much he gives out to all sorts of poor.

53 Other than Demirham, the high heavens had never seen
One more ungodly, but lo, still he knelt,
When close to danger he drew;
But it is too late, then, to try to do good.

54 For he is not motivated by goodwill,
But by his close-approaching doom.

2. Demirham's.

3. Ali was Mohammad's son-in-law, and his prestige in Islamic history is second only to that of Mohammad himself.

Let men always do good, if they wish,
To find God's reward at the ready.

55 While the two soldiers were preparing for battle,
Meanwhile Zrínyi Miklós stood at the ready,
So that some scheme the Turks would not undertake,
As was custom for pagan enemies.

56 Finally he opens great Sziget's gate,
To the gate accompanies his good servant,
With many noble words he refreshes his spirit,
As entourage gives him two hundred swords.

57 Vid goes before them, like a galley upon the sea,
Whose many sails billow in the sky,
For terribly the ostrich feather in his helm
Is moved by the whirlwind, his lance spins in his hand.

58 From elsewhere Demirham, like an Eastern dragon,
Nourished by poison and bearing stoked fire;[4]
A thousand horsemen come, a thousand cavalry with
    these,
Comes Amirassen also with twenty hundred Saracens.

59 The emperor himself from a hill looks down:
What do the Saracen and the Christian knight.
He already considers Vid dead, for Demirham
Had made the emperor believe that it would be so.

60 When Demirham came close to Vid,
With loud voice called to him thus:
"Good health, Deli Vid, Croat knight!
Why so late do you keep your promise?"

4. This quatrain was rearranged significantly for ease of translation.

61 Thus answers Deli Vid: "I came not late;
I am here now, you sent for me now;
But perhaps God will grant me still today,
That you will regret having called me out at this time."

62 "You yourself do not know, Deli Vid, what you speak,
For already you believe me dead.
On your hands, feet I see how greatly you fear:
Rightly, too, for your soul will perish in hell."

63 Thus said Demirham, but Vid like so:
"Pagan dog, hell is not my home;
But I did not come to debate with you,
But let it be revealed, what the two of us know."

64 After such words quickly he charges upon him,
Beneath him the black earth greatly shudders,
Like lightning, his lance flies
From his hand, but Demirham quickly jumps aside.

65 But he was still not so quick as that swift lance,
For the armor on his side it shreds apart.
The Turk rips the lance from his armor,
And his own throws at Vid, unreadily.

66 That was stopped in Vid's shield, harmlessly.
Then swords appeared in the hands of both;
Those two great weapons; so many fiery sparks,
Ars, Mars,[5] fly between them.

67 Sometimes they come together, sometimes fly apart,
Like gleaming, fiery balls from cannons shot,
Which meet in midair:
So act these noble knights.

5. Ars is the personification of skill, Mars the Roman god of war.

68 Beneath a great sword Demirham blows fire,
Does not give Deli Vid any respite,
But Vid does not sleep either, for he has come close
At every opportunity, and wields well his sword.

69 But now the Saracen rises to his feet,
Like a noontime demon,[6] grows greater,
By his hand, the heavy sword lifts high,
From where it falls swiftly upon Vid's head.

70 Like terrible thunder, it crushed Vid's helmet to dust,
And broke also his wrathful head,
Because of which he let himself fall,
Because of which he let both his hands fall.

71 Then with joy the Turkish legion shouts,
The end of Deli Vid's life, it knows, is near,
Among the Christians, however, falls sorrow;
But quickly fortune reverses itself.

72 Deli Vid awoke, took his scimitar in hand,
Cleaved the Turk's gleaming shield in two,
And with that blow wounded his side;
With the second blow broke his helmet.

73 Nor does he allow the Turkish knight to rest,
Renewed, he renews his powerful hands'
Furious attacks. The Turks fear,
Demirham's friends tremble.

74 Demirham, this would be your last hour,
If the Turk could keep his oath,

6. A demon whose power was thought to wax and wane according to the position of the sun; his power was greatest at noon. Cf. Psalm 91:6.

But he does not keep his faith, nor his word,
Here, now, again breaks his sworn promise.

75 When Amirassen sees his companion's situation,
That in terrible battle Demirham is losing,
And Vid on the other hand is growing more powerful,
To the Turkish armies thus he shouts:

76 "Does it not grip your noble hearts,
That with many forces, we sacrifice one soul?
Perhaps we have put down our old manliness,
Or do we not outnumber the infidel forces?

77 Hardly do a hundred of us have a single opponent,
Still this shameful duel we watch.
Thus we make Deli Vid worthy,
And maybe even count him greater than us.

78 Ah, let not these dogs see Sziget!
They who with Deli Vid came to watch battle,
That afterward they may never boast
That amidst our fury, they returned to their castle."

79 So saying, his good horse Karabul he turned,
His personal brigade rallied to himself,
Vid from the back with great strength he attacks,
But because of his speed cannot throw his lance.

80 Deli Vid, seeing this, grew afraid in his heart,
For he sees encircled around him the Saracen legion.
I said that he was afraid, but not that he was frightened,
He did not cower, though he saw the end of his life.

81 He grabs Karabul's brake rein
With his left hand, raises his sword with his right,

Amirassen's neck cuts in two,
And throws his body dead, to the side.

82 Demirham wonders at this occurrence,
For (it must be admitted) it was not by his desire.
Vid however cries: "You have broken your faith,
Pagan cur, you have denied your God.

83 But God will deny you, Demirham, too,
Finally He gives your life into my hand."
Demirham would answer, but he cannot now,
For he is caught up with the rest.

84 He is ashamed and grows red, and tries to hold back
The Turkish forces; but if he cannot be heard
Amidst the great shouting, uselessly he tires
Himself there.[7]

85 Deli Vid, however, like a lithe squirrel,
Leapt astride Karabul, and plows through the brigade.
By now the Turkish army had blended
With the two hundred soldiers who stood by Vid.

86 Gyamer with a great blow cuts off Sár's head,[8]
Who, amidst cries, exhales his soul into the dust.
Kenan kills Palikutya, but János kills Mehmet,
Eivash, Bahtiar, Pirkuch, Bekzade.

87 Yahia Zaim also because of Pál his life
Sends beneath the earth, but Pál's throat

7. This line was deliberately truncated by the author.

8. The word here is actually nonsensical. Either it is extraordinarily obscure or a typographical error; the latter is likely, as it is remarkably close to the word for "head."

Opens Beriel's scimitar, and his blood
It cruelly tastes, and leaves his life there.

88 When the Sziget's Zrínyi bán sees this,
That the emperor is not constant in his word,
With five hundred swords he goes forth and in armor,
He himself bravely brings help.

89 The Turks saw him from afar,
As a sailor sees a perilous gale across the ocean;
They flee before him shamefully,
Each thinks only of himself, not his companion.

90 Deli Vid, however, when he himself surrounded
By countless Turkish forces sees,
His sword is of no use, he knows in his head,
So he quickly arrives at such a plan in his heart:

91 From a dead cavalryman he takes off a helmet,
That, feather and all, he puts on his own head,
He flees also, as the armies carry him,
Before Zrínyi, wherever fate directs him.

92 Zrínyi, however, carries his great spear in the back,
As a sailing-galley its heavy mast,
"Deli Vid! Deli Vid!" he cries with great voice,
But Deli Vid now can give him no answer.

93 "Where, dear servant, Deli Vid, where are you?
Do you live? Or has a Turkish scimitar consumed you?
Answer, if you live!" So walks among the soldiers
Zrínyi; tears gather in his eyes.

94 He thought that they had killed Vid,
Therefore his heart fell into great sorrow.

After the fleeing Turks he bitterly flies,
Alone he is caught up with them.

95 Who will give me such wisdom, that I may write this thing,
What terrible battle Zrínyi waged?
How before him pagan bodies toppled,
As straw before a fire, so suddenly they fell.

96 And you are the first, Kassum Kapidjia,
Whose life Zrínyi bán takes away,
Afterwards Balbazan, Pirkuch, and Kahrina
Their own blood and souls into the dirt vomit.

97 Among dead bodies he walks, like vengeful death,
He wades through Turkish blood, like a boulder in the ocean;
No one before him with weapons can stand,
But the death-bringer cannot find his friend among them.

98 But now Olind bég is ashamed of his flight,
Seeing his captain's death there,
He turns therefore toward Zrínyi his face,
Firmly grips his great sword in his hand.

99 He collides with Zrínyi, but to no avail,
For before him dead on the ground he falls.
His bitter soul flies beneath the earth,
And Zrínyi mercilessly turns elsewhere.

100 He cuts down Hajda, Mussa, Bajazet,
Large-bodied Murtuzan, well-armed Rechep,
Finally he cuts off Aigas basha's head,
With a great dark cloud shrouds his life.

PART TWELVE

1 Deliman is in hiding, with a companion:
Great worries he carries with himself everywhere,
He struggles against his sorrow's colossal tide,
He walks a foreign land, laden with courage.

2 He sat once in the dewy dawn
Atop a particularly fine hill in the breezy shade,
Before him appeared Cupid in full regalia,
Who such fierce words said to himself:

3 "Has my might waned so,
That this man I cannot break?
Perhaps my arrow and bow are not so strong
As they were when my arm triumphed over Mars?

4 But, as I have heard, this one is no inferior of Mars,
Indeed, all his attributes are greater than his;
Now, I will see, how keen is my prowess,
If on your fine personage my arrow makes a mark.

5 Your wound has healed, which it had made before,
But now this new one brings you death;
Never will you forget beautiful Cumilla,
As long as you live, the emperor's daughter."

6 After this he pulled his many arrows from the quiver,
The cruel god-son, and examines his steel;
Gazes upon the anger and despair of all,
His secret, awful power to wound.

7 From among them, he chooses a terrible one,
Which was in great yearning steeped;
Weeping and sorrow are its sharpened barb,
Fleeting beauty was its shaft and feather.

8 This pierced the heart of Queen Venus,
Ruined the joyful spirit of the goddess,
When she saw the death of beautiful Adonis,
And cleaned the youth's wounds with her hands.

9 This he placed in his bow and drew it back to his ear,
And released it into the heart of powerful Deliman;
The arrow invisibly pierced his heart,
All poisonous miseries it left in its center.

10 O, how often came to you in that hour
Cumilla's beautiful eyes, in your deepest thoughts?
How often did the name "Cumilla" come from your lips,
Great Praecopita,[1] in just one moment?

11 If the nightingale listens to your cries,
Your sorrow it would compare to its own,
If its eyes glimpse dawning skies,
Cumilla's beauty it thinks greater.

12 If a stream runs, or a pretty dribbling creek,
His eyes, like they, also run;
If the gentle breezes rustle through branches,
His sorrow too is restless.

13 And thus he calls to himself: "Cumilla! Cumilla!
Why do you make me unhappy?
These countless sighs, which my heart gives birth to,
Why does your unyielding soul not hear?

1. "One from Perecopia"—the seat of Deliman's power near Crimea.

14 Why, from my wailings, do you not soften?
And do not see my sunken eyes, how they swim in tears?
You, however, probably gain strength from my misery,
And of my agony you know nothing.

15 The shining sun itself and this bright sky
Without you are for me thick darkness,
And the meadow's flowering diversity
Is for me boredom and great bitterness.

16 The goldfinch's song, the finch's mourning,
Without you, for me are like the hooting of owls;
Swaying breezes, gurglers' flowing,
As stormy battles, and the flowing of Lethe.

17 Ah, only your beautiful eyes comfort me!
Every rage they calm in me.
But perhaps I deceive myself in this,
Perhaps you hate me, Cumilla, my sweet, beautiful gem!

18 Rushtan bég's death, from which my hands are bloodied,
Perhaps makes me abhorrent in your eyes?
But rather, why would you begrudge that I killed him,
Having saved from that dead dog your beauty?[2]

19 See, now, I will go to you: take revenge on me!
By your hands let me be divorced from my spirit.
But it cannot be, that in so fine a face
Could live cruelty, and that Deliman would come to harm."

20 Thus spoke the Tatar, and jumped on his horse,
Thought he, his many sorrows he might all abate;
Falsely, for the little god leapt into his saddle,
Before him, and in his hand took the guiding rein.

2. Another reference to Rushtan's impotence.

21 Love's god leads Deliman
To where he means to burn him in great fire;
To Landor-Fejérvár[3] therefore he accompanies him,
In Cumilla's lap he drowns him.

22 But Cumilla's heart, likewise
He now pierces with a blind arrow.[4]
She too, like a deer who prances in the forest
When wounded in the breast by a hunter's arrow:

23 So burns Cumilla from love's poison
For she has been wounded by the god Cupid,
She fidgets, either paces, or stands, or sits,
To a confidant speaks thus from her heart:

24 "Fati, my sweet mother, what dark shadows
Stalk my mind; truly, I shall faint;
What a fine guest I see in our lands,
He shoots fire into me, from which I burn.

25 Either Mars, dressed in the small god's fire,
Or Cupid in Mars' fierce armor;
Deliman resembles both in body,
Maybe he defeats both in beauty.

26 Which god moves now my thoughts,
That I should love him, who has killed my husband?
But unhappy me, I love my destroyer,
Or perhaps Deliman hates me, too.

27 Perhaps he hates me because I was Rushtan's partner,
And I love him, because he freed me

3. Probably Nándor-Fejérvár, or Belgrade.

4. To ease translation, "heart" has been moved from the second line to the first.

By his noble hand. Ah, Deliman, my heart!
I, too, was bored by pagan Rushtan.

28 O, how often I desired my life's end,
That I should not lie next to that dead dog!
How often I pleaded to holy Mahomet,
That from his despicable bed I may be freed!

29 Fate has realized this. But who will tell you
That meek Cumilla loves you?
Fati, my sweet mother, I lose my mind,
Perhaps alongside it, my tired life."

30 Thus spoke Cumilla. But her august nurse
Instead of medicine gave her poison.
She thought up masterfully crafted words
With which to strengthen her mood.

31 "O, god Cupid! Great is your power,
For your arm rules over all things,
A king is not great to you, nor is an emperor your lord;
All beauty and honor bring you tribute.

32 A finer soul in a finer body has never been caught on this earth,
Than in yours, Cumilla, my sweet daughter;
But beauty does not bring courage in anything;
Beauty surrenders, if it sees Cupid in arms.

33 In the name of wisdom it is fought against
By many in the world, and they think not,
That in the end, bitterly, its strength
They will find in power over them; that which is held by the tiny god.

34 Then, lost, they try to flee to all corners of the earth
Like an arrow-shot bear wanders about its cave,
And finds no succor. Cupid laughs at such sport,
And executes his vengeance on the fool.

35 So why would you waste uselessly
Your fine youth, and to what end?
Does not this blue sky, which we see on high,
Share with us its beauty, and is happy with it?

36 Does not this bright sun, that which is more beautiful than all else,
Disperse light freely among us, that which we live in?
If the earth were to conceal its goodness jealously,
This world would be lost quickly.

37 The good and the beautiful God has decreed
To be for others' benefit, and men who have withheld
Their good from others, have defied the will of God,
And futilely planted it in the earth.[5]

38 You need not flee from Sir Deliman,
Whose fame has spread beyond the Red Sea,
In whom beauty and honor have made their home;
A better husband you could not ask of Allah."

39 Thus spoke Fati, poured oil on fire;
Cumilla tossed her purity aside,
Nor the great emperor, her father, respected,
Into a small letter poured such words, mingled with her tears:

5. Apparently, a reference to the parable of the talents; cf. Matthew 25:14–30 and Luke 19:12–27.

40 "You will wonder at my forwardness,
Noble Deliman, which I myself acknowledge,
But if God, to whom I belong,
Has so commanded, do not wonder, this is my firm excuse;

41 Therefore understand me thus: as with an invincible
Hand the merciful God has blessed you,
And you have might over all your enemies,
Therefore I too go as a slave before you.

42 But if you only show your might to those
Who as enemies fight against you,
You will not then harm this wretched head of mine,
Which respects, which reveres, which worships you.

43 If you hate me, if me my spouse's sin
Has partially tainted: let Deliman not have pity,
And let there be so much ferocity on his sword;
Let the maiden Cumilla die from him.

44 But if my maidenhood for you have kept
Diana's companions, the pretty nymphs,[6]
Take it gladly: and if not, then keep me still a slave;
Command Cumilla, your servant."

45 Thus she wrote, and sent by a young page,
Awaited with heavy heart Deliman's answer,
Her solace, she believes, may only come from that.
Deliman sent a letter in answer thus:

46 "I see, that truly have I served my god,
That today I may see my better half,

6. Apparently, Rushtan's impotence was such that Cumilla remained a virgin.

The conquered has conquered the conqueror,[7]
Therefore before you I bring myself as a slave."

47 Not long did Deliman delay afterward,
He goes to Cumilla, carrying in his heart
Great joy, and wishes to be there soon,
There, where Cupid's net is cast.

48 O, how ignorant is man's mind!
If one knew what would be his future,
Many of his actions he would surely avoid;
Deliman surely Cumilla would avoid.

49 You two run after each other, like fortunates,
But you both will in time be unfortunate.
See, what horrifying threads the Parcae weave for you,
Once and for all by this your happiness will be torn asunder!

50 What shall I say about their union:
Romantic youths' many romances?
They redouble their kisses around each others' mouths,
Their hearts rejoice over Venus's victory parade.

51 As ivy enwraps a tree
As a snake winds about a pillar,
As Bacchus's vine leans on a post,
In so many ways did the two phoenixes, entangled, sway.

52 Listen further, my Muse. In the Turkish camp
Among many alien people there is a great clamor,
For many thousands of Turks are without captains;
Only the *kajmekan* walks about them.

7. I.e., the conquered (Cumilla, conquered by love) has conquered (with love) the conqueror (Deliman, who conquers in military affairs).

53 All the cruel Tatars, all the daring Saracens,
Many feet, and many strong hands, but all without a head;
The proud Turks likewise
Have lost all their commanders and bashas now.

54 You would not see them among them, only secretive whispering,
Many numerous lamentations, mingled with fear;
Some mourn Idriz, Olind, some Aigas,
All of them their own commanders and their great harm.

55 And they begin to come together in groups,
Now toward the evening, all types of peoples;
Turks, Tatars, Getas, Saracens,
One among them thus begins calling to them:

56 "Truly, must we forever be blind,
Or blindfold our eyes to our danger?
Is it honor, if we fall like fools,
And honor the infidels with our blood?

57 The emperor is aged in his mind,
He has bound himself in his foolhardiness;
He says that he will enter Sziget by force,
Even if not a Turk remains alive.

58 What will he do with the fortress, what with the emperorship,
If this he furiously wishes to fulfill;
But why do I even speak, if indeed,
He thinks naught of Turkish blood spilling?

59 Commanders and bashas and hardened knights,
Those wounded by great Zrínyi's sword,

How many thousand Muslims lie beside him,
Prey to crows and Christian curs?

60 Has his heart been moved by all these?
Has he shed one tear for all these men?
No, no, but has become even crueler,
All of us at once he would glady waste.

61 Now comes the Magyar king against us in great force:
Who goes before us in ordered rank?
The emperor will be in the tent with the cunning *kajmekan,*
What will we do, headless, with hands and feet?

62 But all our troubles we could forget,
If Sir Deliman we could see before us,
Neither from Germans nor Magyars would we then fear,
And in all things we would find fortune.

63 But who forbids us, that we would retrieve him,
Even against the emperor's will, our shining moon?
Let us, half the camp, go to find him,
With our request we could retrieve him."

64 With such stormy words spoke Deriel,
All elect him as ambassador,
That he would go after Deliman with ten thousand,
And wherever he finds him, would bring him back in honor.

65 But the wise emperor, when he hears about this,
In his wise heart is dispirited,
He sees that the common people sully his majesty,
He considers deeply in his thoughts.

66 "O, how fickle is the masses' mind,
It is carried on the slightest breeze of fortune.

Today it displays happiness, if its lot is good,
If tomorrow it is displeased, it will turn to anger.

67 Worthiness, which is the pillar of strong rule,
Is now crushed under the foot of the evil gutter-masses;
Deliman they recall, against me,
But perhaps this too may have a cure.

68 It is better, therefore, that I do not contend with them,
But send an emissary to Deliman.
I will send, and not they, and thus in such way
I will act, and my worth will remain with me."

69 Thus decides the emperor, and thus acts,
Sends Ferhat bég for Sir Deliman,
And the great discord is calmed
By the wise *kajmekan* and cunning Halul bég.

70 Ferhat goes hurriedly, and finds Deliman
Together with Cumilla in fine Fejérvár,
Therefore he puts on all his intelligence,
The emperor's message putting forth in such words:

71 "O noble father's even nobler son!
O Mahomet-faith's most beautiful flower!
The emperor bows his head in greeting,
He who is lord of all things on the earth, over the earth.

72 He bows his head to you, and sends this to you:
Where is your blood which spurs you to honor?
Where is your great fame and name purchased by infidels' blood?
Perhaps you are willing to lose all these?

73 Now Sziget's fortress is in decline,
Even Zrínyi himself has now fallen into despair,

Can you bear not to be present at such a trial?
And your noble hands not to dip in blood?

74 This palm holds its branch to you,
Yours, and no one else's, will be the reward,
The emperor will be content to crush underfoot
Zrínyi, who is the infidels' greatest knight.

75 Cumilla, too, he gives you with both hands,
For he does not want to thus oppose God.
Rushtan's death, too, he boldly forgets;
He, who himself was playing with danger.

76 You the camp with one will awaits,
Turks and Saracens, not only Crimean Tatars,
Come then with us and delay no longer,
Emperor Suleiman can hardly await you."

77 The cruel Tatar's heart softened,
When he heard praise directed at himself;
For he longed for the emperor's misery,
So that he would call him back in glory.

78 Here and now the emperor's affairs he sees in such trouble,
That without help he is in ruin;
Therefore, bravely he decides in himself
That he will go to the Turkish camp to help.

79 Elsewhere, what can do, and how weeps
Beautiful-eyed Cumilla, whose heart burns;
Terrible futures her mind ponders,
Finally before her lord she opens thus her mouth:

80 "O cruel one, why depart you for the Turkish camp?
Do you know, that it is one step away from the grave?

Either the emperor, or another finds in your death
A means of executing vengeance.

81 Is such my lord, like a little chickadee,
Who a flute can so easily lure to dance?
Believe, believe, my lord: Siren's song
This is, which Ferhat now speaks to you.

82 The emperor has lost his army under Sziget,
Now with your loss he wants to be rewarded;
He wants to make prey out of your noble head,
And wants thus to make an end of the tragedy.

83 Either he must not anger his lord,
Or, if he does, must far avoid him,[8]
A grudge they cannot forget,
They entice, they sing, but you must not believe.

84 But from danger, I see, you do not fear,
Fortune's fickleness you think as nothing;
My heart, my soul, where do you put me,
If you encounter danger without luck?

85 You say that you love me more than yourself,
The proof of this rests in only one thing:
Guard your life, on which stands mine,
If the oak falls, the ivy cannot stand.

86 Now I see truly, not for my love
Did you kill Rushtan, but out of cruelty,
Monster, again you think not of Cumilla,
Instead of her, you desire pagan blood.

8. Cumilla here adresses Deliman in the third person, implying both formality and submission.

87 Monster, if you only desire blood in your mind,
Open my breast: there is blood in it;
Drink, do not thirst; my ill fortune
Can never be less than this.

88 But that after your death I should gaze upon your wounds,
To glimpse and count your empty veins:
Do you know, that this could be the last hour of my life?
And is this my hand not enough, to open my own heart?"[9]

89 What should the Tatar do? Honor calls him here,
Cumilla there; like coal, his heart burns;
Within him fights two great foes,
Of which finally wins honor.

90 And so he says to his partner: "O, my heart, my gem!
O, my light, O, my better half!
Wipe your face, and do not mourn me,
Do not foretell evil, I pray, for me.

91 You think me only half a man, if you fear for the infidels for me,
And if you would have me fear Zrínyi's sword,
I do not fear the emperor's cunning
When I may ask counsel of my sword.

92 Do you know, that I have never even seen Zrínyi?
You must know, that I have even been inside Sziget.
Alone I chased thousands as well,
Even so, Mahomet has kept me thus far.

93 On our foreheads is our destiny written,
One may avoid and flee, but no one can escape

9. To commit suicide.

From death; from among a thousand one is left alone
By fortune, whom God has chosen for something else.[10]

94 Not cruelty, believe me, brings me
To such trials, nor blind daring,
But precious honor draws me with its strength;
Let it be, if it must be, my life's end.

95 How you fear, my dear Cumilla:
So you shall rejoice, when you see upon me
Trophies which I have taken off Zrínyi by hand,
And his faithless corpse thrown to the dogs."

96 What shall Cumilla do and with what sort of strength
Divorce Deliman from his purpose?
She can do nothing, but in thick clouds
Sees her pleas fly away.

97 Therefore reluctantly she prepares for the trip,
Though Deliman's future she knows,
Her pretty knees to the ground bows with great weeping,
And thus to the great God begged:

98 "Lord of the heavens, what have I sinned against you,
That so severely you must punish me?
Perhaps my innocence spurs your anger,
Perhaps your eyes cannot look upon your creation.

99 You struck Enceladus[11] with your terrible thunder,
Ixion[12] you tore apart with eagle's talons,

10. This stanza has been rearranged significantly to ease translation.

11. One of the giants of Greek mythology, who was killed by the goddess Athena when he warred against the gods.

12. A king from Greek mythology who was brutally slain by Zeus.

Small tortures, if I compare those to my own;
It is no agony, when only the body suffers in patience.

100 I believe that maybe you are not a sadistic god,
If to your godhood does not belong "cruel"
As a title; then why for me a greater
Agony do you seek, and why do you not kill me now
immediately?

101 For there is no pain in my able body,
Though I would have it torn in Prometheus's place,
But my suffering is in my beleaguered soul,
Agony greater than all forbearance.

102 My youth I wasted beside a corpse,
From death to life only now have I risen,
When my noble lord I obtained,
But fortune now takes that, too, away from me.

103 Therefore I beg of you, you mighty God,
Deliman from such sudden danger
Save, or if against Zrínyi's sword
You are powerless, kill me first."

104 So, departed Deliman with beautiful Cumilla,
Many Turks go before him with great rejoicing.
Not far from the camp at a pretty well-spring
Together with his many companions Deliman stays.

105 Deliman encourages Cumilla, but she
From endless weeping is ever drier.
Sorrow and regret together gnaw at her heart,
Tree and grass in harsh winter are both dry.

106 Cumilla her lord's goblet from his scimitar
Lowers by her hand, and desires to drink of it;

She goes to the well, draws water from the spring,
She knows not, her lord's end will come of it.

107 For with a great dragon he once contended,
And his sword he wished to sheathe;
Into his goblet spilled one drop of blood,
Of which he himself knew not.

108 It was poison; for when Cumilla drank of it,[13]
Her beautiful body was bereft of all strength.
Her life from her body was torturously shut out,
And as she desired, so it was with her.

109 But what does Deliman do at such a scene?
I could not say, though I had a thousand tongues in my mouth;
All Turks, all Tatars he piles dead in heaps,
Shows then his own cruelty.

110 He throws away his sword, tears his clothes,
Naked, he tears trees from their roots;
He does not cry, but roars as like a lion,
Whomever he finds, he kills, destroys, and shreds.

111 Two days and two nights he paces thus the forests,
Then when late he regained his mind,
He takes up his weapons, and dresses in tunic,
For he desires revenge upon the Christians.

13. I.e., the goblet.

PART THIRTEEN

1 God directs the affairs of men,
God has set limits on all things.
But let no man contemplate his passing,
Nor fear, until he reaches it, his ruin.

2 How many battles had the bán seen, and how many dangers?
But his guardian angel had kept him through these;
His hour is coming too, that which farther
Could not have been moved; he must die honorably.

3 Deli Vid walked among the Turks as an enemy,[1]
Among thousands he never met with harm;
Before him, beside him death reaped many,
Him it avoided, or did not find.

4 Many hundreds of thousands of Turks now walked about
him,
There are many in the camp who could recognize him,
But God took the light from their eyes,
Therefore no one took him for Vid.

5 But for him too will come his own hour,
Beyond which he cannot stretch his life,
Confidently he may roam the Turkish camp,
For no one may destroy his life until then.

6 Deli Vid had a beautiful wife,
She among all women alone had stayed in Sziget,

1. I.e., an enemy of the Hungarians—a Turk.

More beautiful than all else was her beauty,
But even above that, her loyalty to her lord.

7 She was a Turkish girl, but Vid by force
Brought her from a fortress in great and terrible battle.
Haissen she was called in Turkish tongue,
But baptism now blessed her with Barbála.[2]

8 She, when having awaited uselessly her lord,
With many tears soaked her spouse's empty bed,
Does not know whether her noble lord is alive
Or, if from the Turks, had suffered glorious death.

9 Mars alights in her heart; and not like others, with tears,
Or with a songbird's unending wailings
Only longs for her spouse, but with bravery
Arms herself with her lord's mail.

10 His mail, arms, she puts upon herself,
Her lord's good sword girds to her side,
Mounts a good horse, spear takes in hand,
Her hair and beautiful face cloaks in a veil.

11 And thus, in Turkish fashion she goes out from
Sziget,
She speaks with Turkish tongue to all in the camp,
Here and there she strides, in all corners,
If only her noble lord she could find.

12 She went to the last section of the camp,
There a large Saracen she found before herself:
Gladly he would gallop, but his horse cannot go,
For with his large frame he has tired his horse.

2. "Barbara," a Berber woman.

13 The wise woman sees his hurry,
Thinks, it cannot hurt to ask his purpose;
Stops the Saracen, therefore, with kind words,
Asks what sort of news he carries so swiftly.

14 He, however, answers her hurriedly:
"Do not delay me, I pray, in my journey,
I take news to the emperor, for which in my lifetime
I shall be a lord, but I beg, leave me in peace."

15 "Tell me also" (the woman thus spoke),
"For truly I cannot be to your harm."
Answers the Saracen: "There in a tent
Deli Vid sleeps in Turkish dress."

16 When the pagan mentioned Deli Vid,
You may imagine what transformation took place on the woman's face;
But she fears that the Saracen may take the news back to the court,
She runs after him, and catches him in three strides.

17 With her spear she quickly tosses him from the saddle,
Quickly with her scimitar slices his head off,
Her good horse immediately, like a squirrel, she mounts,
But quickly, many Turks rush after her.

18 Because shouting began, and a great clamor,
Therefore every Turk runs after her,
And poor Barbara can run no further,
Because a rough hand threw her from the horse.

19 A thousand surrounded her; they ask from whence she came?
And what is the reason for the Saracen's death?

She, poor soul, cannot speak, does not know what to do,
She lies that in Al-Cairo she has a house.

20 "There a Saracen killed my older brother,
And has thus far escaped my eyes."
Quickly she finds defenders, who stand by her,
For a beautiful woman's beauty softens all.

21 Some say, she did well, some toward the bég pull her;
But from such cries Vid was not far,
Therefore, quickly he jumps astride Karabul,
He, too, quickly went toward the shouting.

22 Well, as he goes there, he sees his gentle partner,
Hears, too, her bitter weeping;
Imagine his unspeakable sorrow,
Even so, from afar he wisely shouts thus:

23 "Sirs, stand down, for this is my servant,
Several days now she has stolen my arms and horse,
I have searched through the entire camp for her,
Give her into my hand, and into my domain!"

24 Meanwhile, however, a kadia[3] arrived there,
From whom for Vid there came this response:
"There must be proof for this, and she must stand in court;
The law will not take away that which is yours."

25 Deli Vid mourns, and grows angry,
Shouts: "Pagan dogs, I will not be satisfied thus;
Justice and truth are in my scimitar."
Then he cut Malkuch in two at the waist.

3. A Turkish judge.

26 Abel and Izmail he laid out on the ground,
The Kadia's head he split in two,
He opened a path for Abaza's soul in his chest,
Yakul he laid to eternal rest.

27 Eiuz grabbed his beautiful wife,
But Deli Vid's sword cleaved his body in two;
There he takes his lover by hand,
Took her on his good horse and hurries to leave.

28 Karabul, like a bird, marks no marks on the ground,
But like a screaming arrow, flies so swift,
He could have run across the ocean
And not have known that his hooves are wet.

29 The Turks see that beautiful prey into Sziget
Is being taken on galloping horseback, and recognize Vid,
Vainly they run their horses after him,
For as a light fog, he vanishes himself.

30 Zrínyi welcomes him into Sziget with joy,
For until now he thought him dead.
Vid studied hard the Turk's affairs,
Which he laid out before his lord.

31 But though the noble bán knew all these,
And saw with his eyes his obvious danger,
He fears nothing, but his quick mind
He turns toward the pagan's demise, and his great heart.

32 Elsewhere Suleiman grew merciless,
Against his own blood brought a cruel law.
Said he to himself: "Truly a hundred nations
I have crushed under my foot, and a great part of the world.

33 Perhaps Mahomet has fattened me with fortune
So that he could glorify Zrínyi with all this,
And that my fame and deeds would become his?
I mastered the world, and he should master me?

34 But Mahomet cheats himself, if my ruin he only
Mocks from heaven; he too will incur harm:
I drag the Muslims down to ruin alongside myself,
From whom will he draw glory afterward, then?

35 If however it must be ruined, let all be ruined,
The whole Turkish renown will still honored
Be, for Suleiman with honor will fall;
The Turkish moon and good name will die with him.

36 But let us hear once more the commanders' advice,
Let them ease still my heart's sorrow."
Then for Sokolovich Mehmet he calls,
Commands him to gather the council.

37 Sokolovich calls the head commanders,
According to rank, he seats each,
With dignity, then he asks their pleasure,
He himself sits before them at their head.

38 Sat in the very front the courageous Deliman,
But his embittered heart is consumed by sorrow;
He knows not what he does, and at the emperor's council
He would not heave one sigh from his mouth.

39 His mournful heart brews clouds,
And his two terrible eyes flood oceans,
Like an iron-mine's bellows is his wide breast,
For often it expels great sighs.

40 Therefore they ask him not, nor does he speak to anyone,
But Al bég must speak beside him;
He, however, was a friend of dead Rushtan bég;
He is wise, but there is no bravery in his heart.

41 "Would that God have granted" (thus he says) "that ill-timed,
We would not have stupidly opened a new council,
But what we have once wrought wisely,
We would have finished by now, courageously.

42 But our council's honor has frayed,
The tongue dares not speak what the mind thinks,
For his free speech Rushtan met his end,
Neither can I expect any different myself.

43 Why needed countless generals be lost?
Because we gave no heed to Rushtan's words.
Why lie here bashas and dead begs?
Because one man destroyed our good harmony.

44 What he himself did, however, we saw well,
Turning about-face, we saw him run toward us,
Those who we thought lions
Became so tame, as before hawks, pheasants.

45 Me, too, he threatens with death, but let him!
But I will truly speak my mind:
We can do nothing now, for on the back of hope
We can no longer build our fortune.

46 Among lunacies, there is none better than the shortest,
So let us too finish ours quickly;
And though ours is long, we stretch it still longer,
And greater destruction and abuse will follow it.

47 Therefore I say this: it would be better honorably,
Before we incur even greater injuries bitterly,
To strike camp and return home,
Rather than lose so many warriors here,

48 (And then after our losses to not even triumph,
But make ourselves the laughingstock of the world).
Or let us leave here him who does not wish to follow,
Let him take, with his forces, that which we dare not."

49 Al spoke brusquely, and though Deliman
Through his speech was in other thoughts,
Still he understood that he was being spoken of;
Leapt up, and spoke thus in terrible fury:

50 "You wag your tongue freely, Al; to what end,
You yourself know not, except my honor;
You would shame me, but it falls on your own head,
The yelping of dogs does not reach the bright heavens.

51 You are first in counsel, but in battle has not seen
Anyone your courage; nor such counsel
Have you given, which would bring respectable good to
 our name;
An infidel could not have said worse.

52 So Deliman ran, so shamefully his back
He turned on his enemies in the emperor's presence?
Where was then Al bég, when Szigetvár
He bravely paced, killing infidels?

53 Not thus did two Badankovicses know me;
Not did Sir Hervoics laugh at me,
Nor a thousand others, who I put below the hard earth,
Every day, every day in this army.

54 Do you boast that you fear me,
False fox, and of so much fear in your heart?
Fear not, for truly with such bad blood
My noble hands I have never contaminated.

55 May your soul live on in you, though you deserve
To burden a poplar tree,[4]
But now I return to your council from here,
And say, let us not consider such disgraces.

56 Let the emperor send forth his naked scimitar,
With it show all nations his wrath,
Here at home let them kill shamefully all those
Who do not carry fire, ladders to the siege.

57 I go, I before all, and with terrible hand
I will destroy Sziget's tower in your sight,
Let a hundred Zrínyis come before me, with iron,
with fire;
But I will oppose them with my courage."

58 Thus spoke the Tatar. The council disbanded,
As hurried to speak against him
No one did, therefore they all arose,
And quickly returned to their tents.

59 Demirham, like a boar, nourishes his shame,
He blows fire from his mouth, cannot find his place,
With a great deed he seeks his absolution,
He seeks to duel with Vid again.

60 And thus he cried to himself: "Where is my good name,
Which through many dangers I long acquired?

4. I.e., to be hung.

It would have been better for me to die because of Vid,
Than to live with the emperor's broken word.

61 But the world saw, it was not my sin,
My steed wanted it, I myself, and my weapon.
But God decreed it otherwise;
Perhaps my fortune will rise again.

62 Either a vulture will alight on my chest,
Or honor on my noble head;[5]
I will not leave Deli Vid to my shame,
I swear on my radiant sword and my life."

63 Thus he goes to the emperor, and thus he says to him:
"Mighty emperor, why is there honor
For the noble warrior? Because he risks
His life for his lord, and never fears it.

64 That which he swears in faith, he himself stands by,
He is honorable, even if he is alone in a wild cave,
Or in a forest, or on a plain, or in a beautiful palace,
His faith he must never leave in ruins.

65 Therefore have I no honor,
Because with Vid my duel I could not carry through.
My lord and my emperor, why did I suffer this?
I swear it would have been better to die at Vid's hand.

66 Why did he mock your seal and your faith,
He who shamefully separated us?
Truly Amirassen[6] sees in the next world
What is the faithless man's reward.

5. Apparently, a Turkish saying.
6. In 11.75–79 he interfered with the duel of Deli Vid and Demirham.

67 Would that with my death I could set it right,
The great crack which has broken our honor!
But as bandages for times past
Cannot be applied, let us grieve in its place.

68 But for Mahomet's sake, only this I ask,
Release me, to face Deli Vid with sword,
For there are between us mortal laws,
Which death judges; let it decide between us, once and for all."

69 Thus said Demirham, but the emperor thinks otherwise,
Because from his aged chest many grave considerations pour;
Finally Demirham he answers with wise words:
"Why do you ask, Demirham, that which your tongue speaks?

70 Consider it well and not with proud heart,
Is this the proper place for a duel?
The Turkish flag has come hence with us,
Should it watch a duel, then go away?

71 You are courageous, we know well, but your courage
You wish to show in a small venue, and your strength;
Little good, small respect can stem from this,
But, however, great danger can come forth.

72 Do you know where the warrior is tried?
Where Szigetvár's tower is broken,
I believe Demirham can there find Vid,
Why therefore does he seek a place elsewhere?"

73 Demirham burns, and does not speak, leaves the camp,
Thinks that Suleiman doubts in him;

Therefore in his heart he decides his course of action:
Alone to the siege, he swears, he will go.

74 The emperor sees he uselessly calls councils
For because of Deliman, twice they have dissolved;
Therefore he called to himself only six,
All wise, faithful, and attentive.

75 One said thus to emperor Suleiman:
"Once more let all of us lay siege,
With fire and iron wreck Szigetvár,
And if then we do not wreck it, let us leave it alone."

76 The other: "We do not need to all be here,
Ten thousand infantry let us dispatch around the fortress,
And ten thousand cavalry let us place well,
All assistance therefore to withhold."

77 Third said thus: "Ali Kurt with balls
May burn the castle, with instruments of fire,
The moat to release by irrigation,
That which cannot flow out, to fill with wool."

78 Fourth truly spoke his mind,
Because he wished to return home:
"Pointlessly the camp wastes time here,
The autumn will bring waters and rain upon us."

79 Fifth spoke thus: "Let us leave in Pécs' fortress
Two thousand infantry, a thousand on horseback,
Which shall keep the Szigetians in their bridle,
So that they may not go anywhere to battle."

80 Sixth advised their return home;
All provide reasons for this aplenty,

Only the emperor does not bow before such talk.
Meanwhile they brought Ali Kurt's body.

81 Csontos's cannons had cut off his head,
The janissaries his body could barely catch.
When the Sziget's army had seen the great tumult,
Two hundred selected swords went out.

82 They ended the life of three hundred Turks,
All the cannons' wheels they cut,
In the fuse-holes they pounded iron pegs;
Guszics and Golemi executed all this.

83 But the emperor is furious, yet he mourns within himself,
Ali Kurt's faithfulness occupies his thoughts;
Hayradin captain-basha as a gift
Presented him to the emperor, deeply commending him.

84 Now he had no greater artillery master
Who could watch over the fires;
Therefore quickly he moved from anger to distress,
Sziget will stand, he believes, to his shame.

85 Now he begins to consider retreat,
Only deliberates how he could go in peace,
Knows well that a lion stands behind him,
Because of whom, a single step he cannot take peacefully.

86 However a pigeon flies out from Sziget,
In a nest in Kanizsa they raised it,
By his wings he hurries there again,
However such a thing happens, accidentally:

87 A hawk from above spies out his prey,
Launches his two swift talons against it,

That, however, sees that it flies in vain;
So in the emperor's tent hides itself.

88 Quickly many bostandjis[7] sieze the pigeon,
And notice a small scrap of paper,
This the pigeon under his wing from Sziget brought;
They took this news in to the emperor.

89 Quickly a Hungarian translator they called in,
The Christian letter gave into his hand.
On the front of the letter such letters are written:
"Give this letter to the Magyar king."

90 "If you ask how we are, we are close to death,
We, to whom reinforcements bring no hope;
Five hundred we remain, but all to the grave
Are closer, by our wounds, than to the world.

91 But neither can those pagan dogs boast about us;
A sixth of the camp we have put under the sword,
Generals, bashas, many we have killed,
Now just a headless foot is our enemy.

92 Within two days comes our final hour,
For the dragon has wreathed his fangs about us.
Even then, what our Christian effort can do,
Gladly we will show to this world.

93 Most of all they like to destroy us by fire,[8]
For which we find refuge nowhere;
We plan to end our lives out there,
We think it a waste to lose our lives by fire.

7. The imperial bodyguards.
8. I.e., cannon fire.

94 Of our relief give no thought,
For it is impossible, we see ourselves;
But you can do great injury to the pagan Turks,
If you go after them with your army and yourself.

95 For they cower, for they have no general.
Lost are their wise men, and their captain;
The emperor and the *kajmekan,* only these are strategists,
Deliman, Demirham are daring fools.

96 Twenty-five thousand Turkish dogs lie here,
Which in ten sieges came against us fearfully.
More we do not write, but in health
May God keep your Highness in good providence."

97 When Suleiman heard this thing,
That Sziget's hope was at an end,
He took heart in himself, and that in vain
The pigeon's flight would not be, released it.

98 Traitorous bird, where is your faithfulness?
Will you fly, or have you no shame?
You betrayed your master, his secret letter
Dropped into the hands of the pagan enemies.

99 But it does not rejoice for long in its freedom,
For the hawk all this time watched it from above.
Flies after it, and catches it by its wing,
With his merciless claws glories in its shredding.

100 The emperor to all quarters orders a siege,
That everyone would take either fire or iron;[9]
Some take sulfurous grenades dipped in pitch,
Ten thousand fiery grenades are distributed.

9. I.e., either a gun or a sword.

PART FOURTEEN

1 Here comes Zrínyi's shining star,
Here his immovable lodestar,
The bán's deeds my hand writes,
Which the Spirit of God has breathed into my mind.

2 His ship will not cruise into danger
Who wisely uses this star as guide;
Faithfulness and nobility are his magnetic pole,
He who does not let this star disappear.

3 My compass now guides me into port,
Fortuitously I have crossed the sea,
I begin to recognize my friends on the shore,
Who came with great joy before me.

4 From afar I recognize courageous Mars's son,
I see, I see how he drives his horse;
He, my noble brother, all Magyar, all Croat;
Truly, we see, he loves his country.

5 The eye that looks to the sun sees the falcon's son,
By his talons we recognize the lion;
Courage tests Zrínyi's true son,
Who can break away from neither one.[1]

6 I believe it is Zrínyi Péter[2] who my eye sees,
Who terrifies Bosnia and Herzegovina;

1. From either of his countries.

2. Péter Zrínyi (1621–1671) would go on to translate the epic into Croatian, the year after Zrínyi published it in Hungarian.

We have seen already his trial of courage,
Which with mind, arm, and heart he executed upon the
Turks.

7 But woe, a great hound steals after him!
What furious envy seethes from his throat!
It is indeed envy, though it is not in its power
To harm him, because of his noble nature.

8 Fear nothing, brother, for the great heaven sees
That nobility's shadow is envy;
This is the inheritance of our ancestors,
Which cannot be broken until the world reaches its end.

9 Know that they lunge at us with venomous huge fangs,
But not just Turks, for there are other beasts also,
Who gnaw, like rust corrodes strong iron,
But leave alone, lest their teeth they destroy.

10 I see from elsewhere our nation's pillar,
Sir Veseléni[3] rides his good horse,
Grave concerns are on his mind, for grave troubles are
upon him,
For he sees our country in a downpour indeed.

11 I see Bottyáni[4] also, with his shoulders the nation
Supporting, and not letting it slip into ruin,
And though he expects from no one a reward,
He draws enough good from his own virtue.

3. Ferenc Wesselényi (1606–1667), a Hungarian noble and a good friend of the Zrínyis. After the author's death, Wesselényi, Péter Zrínyi, and Fran Krsto Frankopan led an unsuccessful uprising against Hapsburg rule in Hungary and Croatia.

4. Count Ádám Batthyány (1610–1659), a member of the famous Batthyány family and a friend of the Zrínyis.

12 I see a hundred others whom gladly
I would greet, but to whom I now bow head,
For I have left far behind my history;
Now I must begin it over.

13 A Turk, filled with time, was in the army:
His origins were in wide Egypt,
In his mind was horrific knowledge.
His name, however, was great Alderan.

14 Alderan, who ruled horrific spirits,
All the elements and the great mists,
The heavenly planets, earthquakes,
Great lightnings, striking thunder.

15 This stepped in to the emperor, thus began to speak:
"My coming to you, you will marvel at,
But understand its reason, for I will be of use,
For upon your foes I will send harm.

16 Terrifying spirits I hold enchained,
Some I release only for others' injury;
All the hells are under my domain,
With these the infidels, if I wish, I can destroy.

17 Therefore fear nothing, and prepare no arms,
Only wait peacefully a little while,
Upon Sziget I will bring a terrible cloud,
Sulfurous flames, and all demons.

18 You will see what use will be their God, their Jesus,
If I fall upon them with my knowledge;
But lo, before I tell you more,
I shall bring up great Ali, who is their destroyer."

19 Alderan convinces the emperor with such words,
For truly, he proves his word with a terrible curse,
He releases the apparition to freedom,
And he leaves on his black horse.

20 Alderan alights upon his black horse,
Finds a place for himself in a forest clearing,
Twelve Christian youths he secretly
From the camp brings forth, who were bound.

21 The throats of these with a great knife he slices,
Their innocent blood pours in a basin,
His other companions then sends away from himself,
In the great theater spies only himself.

22 It was in that time when Delia
Ignited the god Pan to her love;
When by her moisture into first dreams
Earthly men were dissolved.[5]

23 Alderan a bronze stylus took in his hand,
An occult circle inscribed about him;
He repeats it not far from there in the dirt,
And stands innermost in the middle.

24 Bizarre characters are formed by him
By Christian blood in each circle,
But even so he does not give peace to the dead,
For he quarters four on each of the wheels.

25 The four corners of the earth he declares them,
And by each one places grotesque markers,

5. A complex metaphor: the moon, the goddess Delia, rose to her peak (at which point she was beautiful enough to seduce Pan), and men fell asleep with the onset of the evening dew.

Thus he appeases the hellish spirits,
And thus he begins terrible verses:

26 "Hear, mournful spirits of hell,
Who did not suffer your companions in heaven!
Hear, terrible Acheron gods,[6]
Pluto[7] and Sterapon,[8] and chief princes!

27 Lord of Belbuzel[9] and Harpad[10] and Phlegethon,[11]
Horrific watcher of the flow of Styx and Lethe,
Inexorable army of all Cocytus,
You who fell below the earth from heaven![12]

28 Hear, and come swiftly out of the earth,
Let not one of you remain in the bowel of hell;
That which you savor: its hour is now,
In which the infidel must go to his ruin.

29 War and strife I command upon them,
Great cruelty from you I demand,
Come, therefore, flaming fires of Styx,
Furies,[13] Harpies,[14] hundred Briareoses." [15]

30 But to such words, no movement resulted,
Phlegethon gave no sign of making ready,

6. Acheron is the main river of the Greek underworld; the "Acheron gods" would be the gods of the dead.

7. The Roman god of the dead.

8. Serapis, the Greco-Egyptian god of death.

9. Beelzebub, a "prince of hell" in Jewish lore.

10. Unclear; apparently a Persian god of death.

11. The Phlegethon, Styx, Lethe, and Cocytus, along with the aforementioned Acheron, were the five rivers of the Greek underworld.

12. Cf. Revelation 12:9.

13. Roman embodiments of the rage of the damned.

14. Vicious birdlike monsters from Greek mythology.

15. Hundred-handed giants with fearful strength.

Therefore great Alderan began to grow angry,
Viciously stamps the ground with his foot.

31 Stamps the ground viciously with his foot,
Screams derangedly with his furious mouth:
"So do you still not hear, O you with misery
Laden, tortured spirits, and with great sorrows?

32 You wretched, think you that my tongue
I cannot unleash, and name the name
of him, who in heaven left his godhood,[16]
And who on earth took up the character of a man?

33 Or that I have forgotten the seventy-seven names
Of Him, who threw you down from heaven,
Or his sufferings and innocent blood,
Which he, by your provocation,[17] innocently spilled?

34 And it flowed upon your great fiery fortress,
And saintly spirits, to your anger,
It brought out,[18] and at the right hand of his father
Seated, to your eternal shame?"

35 Barely could Alderan speak these,
Suddenly dark clouds gripped the skies,
Thrice Luciper shook the ground,
And darkened the light of the stars.

16. I.e., Jesus Christ.

17. Christ planned his own crucifixion to expiate men's sins, but in the immediate sense it was caused by Satan's "provocation" through the betrayal by Judas; cf. John 13:27 and John 18:2–3.

18. Before being raised to life three days after the crucifixion, Christ "descended into hell," and according to some interpretations, brought out some of the dead who were there into heaven; cf. 1 Peter 3:18–20 and 1 Peter 4:6.

36 Now the earth's surface they blackened
And the sky too horridly covered,
Tigers, dragons, bloodthirsty hyenas,
Terrible giants and chimeras.[19]

37 There was Tantalus with his table,[20]
Savage Atreus,[21] shamed Lycaon,[22]
Medusa's head with venomous froth,
Awful Eumenides[23] with flaming torches.

38 There Diomedes[24] with his hellish steeds,
Cruel Terodaman[25] with lions,
Terrifying Busiris[26] with bloody altars,
Procrustes,[27] Laestrygonians,[28] monstrously.

19. A monster from Greek mythology with the body of a lion, the heads of a lion and a goat, and a snake's tail.

20. A wicked ruler in Greek mythology who was sentenced to the eternal torture of standing in front of a food-laden table only to have the delicacies retreat out of his reach when he grasped for them.

21. The father of Agamemnon and Menelaus in Greek mythology, who was said to have killed his own father and brother in order to seize the throne.

22. Another wicked ruler from Greek mythology who was transformed into the first werewolf.

23. A Greek name for the Furies.

24. A warrior from *The Iliad,* he owned a pair of horses descended from Zeus's own herd. The "steeds" could also be a reference to how he attacked and wounded Ares, the god of war, while riding in a chariot driven by the goddess Athena.

25. A mythological ruler of Scythia who fed his lions with human flesh.

26. An Egyptian king of Greek mythology who was said to sacrifice any strangers who came to his land.

27. A depraved bandit from Greek mythology who would kidnap wayfarers and place them on his bed, stretching the bodies of those who were shorter and cutting off the legs of those who were longer than the bed.

28. Giant cannibals in *The Odyssey.*

39 There could be heard Scylla's[29] barking,
Cruel Geryon's[30] horrible moaning,
Hellish Mezentius[31] and Phalaris's torture,[32]
A thousand Briareoses, Cerastes,[33] and Hydras.[34]

40 But among all of these grandly strides
World-terrifying, horrific Death.
He conquers all in greatness and repulsion,
Both his hands hold dreadful scythes.

41 So come the spirits, and in thousand other forms,
But who has power to describe it?
Foremost is Pluto on fiery horseback,
Foremost Astragora[35] on sulphurous carriage.

42 Before these, Alderan thus opens his throat:
"Hear, hear Alderan's speech!
Who has stolen the devil's weapon?
Or who has put a dent in his power?

43 Once, I know, you fell from heaven,
And the starry skies eternally lost,
But no one took your weapons,
No one has powerless made you.

29. A monster from Greek mythology, a dragon who lived in a crag opposite the whirlpool Charybdis, and who snatched and devoured sailors passing by.

30. A three-headed giant from Greek mythology.

31. In Roman mythology, a ruler so overwhelmingly cruel that he was exiled from his own land.

32. A historical king of Sicily who was said to possess a hollow bronze bull in which he would shut his victims, light a fire under the bull, and then pretend that their screams were the bull's bellowing.

33. A horned serpent from Greek mythology.

34. A monster from Greek mythology who had nine heads and breathed poison; when one cut off one of the heads, two more grew in its place.

35. Chief of witches.

44 Still, you just shamefully bore it,
When the resurrected man from among you
Brought out the souls; and among you all,
There was none, who could have withstood the cross.

45 All your miseries thereafter stemmed from that,
The gospel was trumpeted, and your eyes on the cross
Dare not rest, and in the bowels of the earth
You cower before it, if it is before you.

46 Lo, if a man suffers a wrong,
He is giving his old nemesis opportunity for more;
Why should his noble heart tremble,
He, who wrought great feats even in heaven?[36]

47 Now, greater wrath falls on your heads,
Heaven has thus destined to your shame,
That all enemies should flee at the sign of the cross,
And that all glory should fall to Christians.

48 It is thus, for a few measly Christians
Have hidden themselves in Sziget against the world's
three parts;
They have hope in nothing;
Only in him who hung, and in his cross.

49 Five hundred times a thousand of us besieged them,
A third of us he left there our precious lives,
Two planks in the shape of a cross humble us,
Us Turks, your faithful ones.

50 Raise, then, your weapons, raise your courage,
Advance on Sziget with brimstone and fire,

36. I.e., why should the demons tremble from God, when they even waged war in heaven?

You must burn it to ashes, the men and the stone,
You must ruin it, and its good name."

51 Here stopped Alderan, but the hell-spirits
Swarmed as one toward Sziget,
But Alderan shouts, commands the earth,
Brings forth great Ali for the destruction of Sziget.

52 The earth is silent, but he stamps it with his foot,
And so he opens his mouth with a great shriek:
"Do you want to countermand me, to your ruin,
Lose my favor by your obstinacy?

53 I, Alderan, command, I who rule the darkness:
And if I wish, the skies drape themselves in clouds,
But if I wish, the clouds fall,
And the airy skies remain clear.

54 If I wish, by my word I enrage the seas,
And when I wish, I calm the foam,
And verily, all winds I command,
All elements await my bidding.

55 You too I can drag down from the heaven,
Gilded moon, if I call you to my assistance;
So also, coffin-dwelling shades
Why should I not command by such power?

56 Come forth, Hazret Ali, come forth from the earth's
bowel!
Bring out great Zulfiqar[37] from your deep grave,
Again you must water your horse from a lake of blood,
The infidels have forgotten of you."

37. The legendary sword of Ali.

57 With a great roar, at such command the earth
Immediately splits itself in two,
Brings forth a knight clad in white velvet-silk,
His head covered with a sheer turban.

58 A brown horse is beneath him, but sorrowfully
He rides the steed in the moonlight,
Once with heavy eyes he looks up in fury,
Sees Alderan with the great circles:

59 "Who wakes me from my agony,
And to greater agony calls my accursed head?"
Thus calls Ali: "Who my resting place
Sought out, and shakes me from slumber?

60 Ah! Greater tortures can men devise
Than sadistic demons can even imagine;
It is greater torture for me now to see the world
Than those that I usually suffer.

61 What do you want with me, cruel Alderan,
That by me you may rejoice in Szigetvár's ruin?
But you, despite your knowledge, will be disappointed;
For truly, my power has been broken.

62 Such Christians do not live in Sziget
Who could be hurt by the Al-Koran's scripts,
Nor by the hellish and encoffined spirits;
Greater than Mahomet is their God.

63 For he will burn with me in eternal fire;
Why did we glory in Christian blood?
God does not take pleasure in the rod of discipline.
We once were, but God has sent us into eternal fire.

64 But these are now different times and different men,
I see that they are much more favorable to God
Than they who were before rebellious;
And they too will fall; but woe to your blood!

65 The three who Suleiman's life cruelly
Spun, the Parkas, will not wait much longer;
Henceforth you will see how they shred it,
And the Furies have come forth to no avail.

66 Indeed, I will be there too, to watch your work,
What usage the demons will bring you,
But that I should draw my Zulfikar, do not expect,
For God so decided to turn it into dust."

67 Thus speaks Hazret Ali, on his terrifying mount
Flies bitterly after the other spirits.
Then Alderan realized within himself,
That with the Christians stands the true God.

68 They fly and arrive in horrific force,
Where Phlegethon had flooded all with darkness;
Where Tisiphone[38] blows her terrible trumpet,
Beelzebub has ordered his army into the dark sky.

69 The Furies rush with horrific torches,
You would think that they will light the earth afire,
Cruel Harpies with monstrous maws,
Bloody venom they spew, loathsomely.

70 Hateful Astragora the gates of the winds
Opened, throwing her spear of lightning,
And frees from their chains those proud necks;
On wings, they search for Sziget.

38. The Fury from Greek mythology charged with avenging murders.

71 Then the night wind calls Eurus[39] to evil,
But he fears nothing of weapons,
Boreas[40] furiously alights on lithe wings;
And all bring brutal peril for Sziget.

72 Rainbow bends his golden bow,
Mightily thunders, as if shooting his arrow;
Proud Orion[41] wields his great sword,
All "to Sziget!" and "to Sziget!" cry.

73 The Christian knights run to the bastions,
But cannot withstand the power of fire;
The flames of the god Vulcan are afoot,
They allow no one close to the bastions.

74 For the Turks, too, with countless fiery shots
Fly as one with the Furies;
The outer fortress they have already taken by siege,
The bán has been forced to the inner keep with five hundred others.

75 But neither can there be much respite there,
For thick fire thunders over their heads,
Countless thousand spirits haunt Zrínyi;
He, however, as a rock, trembles nothing.

76 Thus he says to his men: "Fear nothing,
For by this, God gives us eternal glory.
If a hundredfold more demons bare their teeth at us,
They cannot harm our souls, for God helps us.

39. The Greek personification of the East Wind, believed to bring misfortune.

40. The Greek personification of the North Wind, believed to be the most violent.

41. A legendary hunter from Greek mythology. In this context, placed alongside meteorological phenomena, he is actually the constellation.

77 Hell-born spirits are our adversaries,
Our hope, however, is with God;
For Him, we die with glad and faithful hearts,
Let it be as He hath willed in Himself!"

78 Thus he cries, and so gives himself courage,
And to his terrible, noble band;
Commands then his three chief vajdas,
That in the square they should stand for battle.

79 These, commands to courageously fall on the Turks,
In the outer fortress's square to kill the Turks;
Ghastly spirits blow into their eyes sulfurous fire
In vain, for they walk with courage.[42]

80 There weapon against weapon meets,
Knight with knight also mixes;
In the darkness between them only groans sound,
Terrifying death glories in their midst.

81 Some exhale their spirits through many wounds,
Some release them with much cursing;
The Christians do not drop, but the Turks in heaps;
For once and for all the flower of knighthood will fall.

82 The fire seems to fly on the Christians,
But rather it falls on the pagan Turks,
Saracens and Tatars, Turks, into death
God's will sends, all alike.

83 Mercilessly charges furious Deliman,
Like a roaring lion in the Caspian mountains.
O, how many flames he breathes into Sziget,
How many blows he takes up on his shield!

42. This quatrain was rearranged significantly to allow for sensible translation.

84 A great carbuncle[43] was on his helm,
By this they recognized him even in the dark,
But more than the gem shines his scimitar,
More than his scimitar, his courage.

85 He, as a ravenous wolf at the sheep pen
Tries with his chest to topple the fence:
So strides Deliman also about Szigetvár,
Tries to topple the stone wall.

86 Demirham on the other hand resembles a Fury,
For terrifyingly he twirls his sword,
"Deli Vid! Deli Vid!" he tirelessly shouts,
"Where are you, and why have you hidden yourself?

87 But hide you between walls, or beneath the earth,
Hide, where live the Indus and Garamanta;[44]
Demirham will find you, and your spirit will release
This terrible spear in my hand."

88 Deli Vid can no longer stand such words,
He leaves the battle, and where the Turkish dog barks,
Thence he leaps, and to him shouts thus:
"Pagan, have you ever seen me in hiding?

89 But you are faithless and do not deserve
To have Deli Vid raise sword against you;
For your faith, your word, and your manhood
All together, you have once and for all forsaken!"

90 The Saracen recognized Vid by his words,
He gave a prayer with great despondency,

43. A ruby.

44. The names of two tribes thought to live in India and Africa, respectively; together they imply the farthest reaches of the world.

And thus wisely called to Vid in Turkish:
"I beg that you hear me, Vid, attentively.

91 Both of us are mistaken in our thoughts,
Neither did you hide, nor in my good faith
A dent, or shame did I ever bring;
My anger made me speak of your hiding.

92 If the entire camp broke its faith,
Thinking useless my death,
Am I guilty? You saw me well,
Did you see that I called anyone for help?

93 But this has passed, now is our time;
Come out on the field, let us not delay it any longer,
It will be seen, who are Deli Vid and Demirham;
Let him live, whom his good sword and God allow."

94 Deli Vid would not gladly leave the fortress,
For he does not have such permission from his lord,
But the Turk does not want to leave him alone,
Therefore he courageously leaves with Demirham.

95 O, how sadly leaves behind his lord
Deli Vid, how many tears he sheds for him,
But when Demirham sees his weeping,
Says thus: "Do you so fear to suffer death?"

96 Still weeps Deli Vid, and answers thus in his weeping,
"Idiot, what do you think? That in the presence of fear,
Deli Vid would cry; you are mistaken.
My life, my death I count as but one.

97 Neither one can bring me shame,
In fact, by my death I increase my good fame.

But I weep when good Zrínyi comes to my mind,
He must fall, together with Szigetvár.

98 I see that today that rose-stem will fall,
Who gives such comfort to Christendom,
I see that the sky stands open before him,
And angels await him with joy.

99 And your head is small revenge for this,
Your blood is meager for my thirst;
The entire Muslim nation for one drop of his blood
Can never adequately pay."

100 Demirham smiles, but inside feels otherwise,
For he realizes early his last hour;
His heart foretells terrible thoughts,
Still he bravely steels himself against them.

101 When from Szigetvár they were a good distance,
A pretty round meadow found in a valley;
You would think that it was made purposefully for battle,
Here only two fight a fatal duel.

102 Demirham his anger terrifyingly
Nourishes within himself, draws his scimitar;
But Vid first shouts into the heavens unto God:
"My Lord, see now from the heavens your servant!

103 A Jewish child in the Terebinth valley
Against Goliath you gave victory;[45]
In a burning furnace, joyfully
Shadrach, Meshach, and Abednago gave you praise.[46]

45. See the biblical account of David's killing of the giant Goliath in 1 Samuel 17.

46. See the biblical account of Nebuchadnezzar's unsuccessful atttempt to

104 Lord, let it now be as you will it."
After such words he drew forth his keen blade.
Not far from himself he watches Demirham,
With heavy weapon, how he breathes fire, flames.

105 They clash then so viciously,
As on the ocean if two galleys collide;
He who remains on the water, his heart is glad,
He who sinks, his falls into despair:

106 So now each of the two knights guards himself,
Wields his sword to his companion's destruction;
Both, however, are more ready for death,
Than for showing a sign of slightest fear.

107 But the pagan lifts his sword with both hands,
Striking, cleaves Deli Vid's helmet;
Slashing farther, he injures his side,
So that a red stream he sees flowing from there.

108 Deli Vid does not frighten, he leaps to Demirham,
And with terrible strength strikes his face;
Not vainly does the noble sword fly to the pagan,
It travels from the middle of his nose to his mouth.

109 Then blood and venom erupts from his heart,
He cannot hold himself back from anger,
He tries no longer to duel masterfully,
Again and again, strikes violently.

110 Deli Vid, however, grabs his neck,
With his other hand, opens in many places his flank;

---

kill God's worshippers in Daniel 3. This quatrain was rearranged significantly to allow for sensible translation.

He thrashes in his hands, and roars, not shouts,
From wounds, fury, he cannot even speak.

111 Demirham, like a torch, seeing his end,
Wants to redouble his courage:
From Vid's hand he quickly twists himself,
And with a great blow strikes Deli Vid's neck.

112 He slices through his helm along with his forehead;
No longer can he keep himself on his feet.
He falls, and falling still strikes at his leg,
He wants nobly to end his hour.

113 Vid, however, makes him to fall further,
For his breast with his gleaming sword he forces open,
Then his weeping soul he spews below the earth,
By a terrible shadow his life is darkened.

114 Deli Vid himself can struggle no further,
Just barely he manages to hold in his spirit;
Close to Demirham, he too fell there,
The sky sees his soul, the grass drinks his blood.

Be witness, heavens, for Deli Vid's end,
For with many eyes you watched the last of his life:
To the last drop he gave his blood for his God,
Bear testimony to Deli Vid's end!

PART FIFTEEN

1 The bán sees his last hour approaching,
The entire army he calls to form rank,
Those, too, who had gone out to battle,
Among whom Deli Vid alone stayed there.

2 And thus he speaks to them: "Behold, knights,
The situation you now share with me:
Not just Turks, Tatars bring us now destruction,
But fire, but iron, but all the elements.

3 God tries us in every way,
Just as a master a goldcraft tries in a fire;
And as He sees our faithfulness,
He has prepared us a beautiful diadem in heaven.

4 He is no longer angry with us, for now His punishment
For our sins He has lifted,[1] and His true law
He has fulfilled: now faith's reward
He is preparing in highest heaven, and takes us there.

5 Let us not recoil, then, from going to our deaths,
Which will give us a path to eternal joy;
Today, soldiers, we must lose our lives,
And today all our trials seal.

6 We have lived nobly, let us die nobly,
Give the entire world an example by it;

1. Cf. 1.24.

Today we bring dignity upon our names,
This day gilds all past actions.

7 Pagan curs do not carry us on leash,
The emperor does not parade us, bound, in his victory
procession;
Let the Turks suffer even in our last hour,
Let them see, that God is with the Christians.

8 Because the fire will not let us stay here,
As soon as God allows us to see the twilight,
Let us leave the fortress, and show there:
That which we were in life, we still are now."

9 Thus spoke great Zrínyi, and all the knights
Joyfully his speech received;
Mars flies into all, and their noble eyes
Flash with courage, like gemstones.

10 Deafening noise arises from the soldiers,
Like when a hard breeze pummels a forest;
Each can only hardly await the time,
When he may surrender his soul to God.

11 Shields, breastplates, sword-scabbards:
They throw off themselves all encumberments,
For they desire wounds more than these,
By which they may release their souls to heaven.

12 Zrínyi meanwhile goes to the opulent treasure-store,
All riches he puts in a pile,
Makes a fire under it by a torch,
He surrenders all to smoke, all treasure that he has.

13 One cloak, one coat he alone selects for himself,
Those which were the most beautiful among all of them,

In this he used to present himself at court,
In this at weddings and victory processions.

14 Two golden bracelets he chose then,
With these marked his noble arm,
A heron feather also affixed to his helm,
A hundred pieces of gold split between two halves of his
cloak.

15 Oh, what a wondrous thing, that a reward he guarantees
For his own executioner! What a steely knight is this!
The mention of death is truly sorrowful,
Hector and Achilles trembled before it.

16 But even at death Sziget's Hector,
That he can bravely stare death in the eyes—
Even if it appears in dreadful raiment—
He proves, and how to walk with courage.

17 He lit his treasures, and burned all;
His weapon then he removed from its peg,
From among the countless he grew to love one,
This to his side he nobly affixed.

18 The God sat on His throne,
From whence He watches the world in grace,
Great Dignity, Majesty stand around Him,
His throne is fixed in great eternity.

19 Fortune and Nature humbly
Stand below him, ready for service,
Glory flows before Him in great streams,
Infinite Mercy sprawls as an ocean.

20 Countless glorious souls
Sing "Glory!" magnificently before Him,

The Jewish poet's[2] ceaseless verses
Proceed royally from his harp.

21 The heavenly aria's beautiful appeal
Even fair Echo's reply exalts.
"Holy, holy, holy, almighty God, Jehova!"
All heavenly hosts jubilantly cry.

22 Cherubim, Seraphim hosts rejoice,
Before the holy lamb they humble themselves,
And other hosts in white raiments stride,
They also everywhere surround the lamb.[3]

23 From such majesty verily commands
The good, the true, the great Jehova,
That all music would at once fall quiet,
And that His angelic court should gather.

24 It is as He wills, and gather
All the glorious heavenly hosts;
Humbly they genuflect to God,
And He begins to speak to them thus:

25 "Hear, hear, you swirling skies,
Hear, my faithful, heavenly hosts,
Hear this, land and earth, and waters of the earth,
My speech, and you, great oceans!

26 Foolish audacity you have clearly witnessed,
By which you saw a giant attack me;
The proud thought that a punishment upon him,
Along with his companions, I could not devise.

2. The "Jewish poet" is David, whose "ceaseless verses" are contained in the Psalms.

3. I.e., Jesus Christ; cf. Revelation 12:5–7.

27 Fallen, I blasted him with my heavenly thunder,
And eternally I forced him out of heaven,
He left heaven, but proudly
He still rebels foolhardily.

28 And he is not satisfied with many thousands of souls,
That he has levied a tax on their countless sins;
He dares to molest my faithful,
Who are chosen by me, my beloved.

29 Where the Szigetians battle for me,
And already for my faith have shed much blood,
Hell-born spirits seize upon them,
And desire to beat their true faith from them.

30 And how would it be possible to allow them this?
Being the true God, that I could suffer this?
No, no, but let one legion go arm,
They must once again be committed to hell!

31 Depart, Gabriel, with heavenly host,
Depart to Sziget with mighty armored hand!
There you will find them, but from there expel them,
Destroy them together with their tremendous pride.

32 Watch, then, where are Sziget's warriors;
When they undress their souls of corporeal robes,
On your arms let them come before me,
Here in ordered ranks let them forever be."

33 Thus He spoke, but not with tongue and not by appeal,
But with gleaming godly will;
The angels understand, for with great joy
They agree to God's great will.

34 Gabriel therefore an army with him
Brought on swift wing, and bearing a cross as a standard.
The sky shone, wherever their course
The magnificent army kept, and their flight.

35 Humbly, Rainbow his gate
Opens before them and speaks blessings,
And even the splendid Milky Way ornaments himself,
Seeing the great God's legion of grand angels.

36 The Big Dipper[4] carries their many arms,
Easing the load of the heavenly host,
Arms-bearing Eagle[5] readies his thunder,
By which to throw down the satanic horde.

37 Hercules gives regret, he cannot accompany them;
There may be no vacancy in his spot.
He stands motionless, sentry of the sky,
He stands with his great staff, against the enemy.

38 The eternal legion in the sky halted,
Only Gabriel alone in Sziget landed,
That Zrínyi has prepared for death, he finds,
And likewise that he is imploring God.

39 Before him appeared Gabriel, winged,
Majestic was he in angelic raiment;
His body was clad in royal purple,
His arm with fierce, flaming broadsword.

40 In his other hand a beautiful palm branch
Together with a wreath held aloft.[6]

4. In Hungary, this constellation is associated with a cart, rather than a ladle.
5. Another constellation, associated with Zeus.
6. The palm branch and wreath, symbols of salvation.

In the dark room he brought light;
Gabriel to Zrínyi then spoke thus:

41 "O, beloved servant of the lord of hosts,
Noble flower of all Christendom!
You were JESUS' sanctified general;
Here is the crown of God!

42 This sends you the horde-destroying God,
But another He has prepared, which will rest on your head;
From shining stars it shall be woven forever,
You will bear it in the high heavens.

43 An angelic legion God has sent you
For your relief, with whom you may triumph
Over these, your misery-gorged enemies,
Who have proudly risen from hell against you.

44 Therefore enliven your manly heart,
One last time redouble your courage;
Let not the senile thief see your severed head,
But send his soul below ground first."

45 Thus said the angel and enlivened him,
Called the heavenly host down from the sky;
Not far saw Luciper and his forces,
The archangel before him called thus:

46 "What are you doing here, O you wretched ones,
O, greatly tortured and proud ones!
Perhaps you do not see the world's God,
Who with His great thunder has armed against you?

47 It has been willed in the secrets of God,
That they who die now in Szigetvár

Should go with us to the kingdom of God;
Why then do you wait here in vain?

48 Depart, accursed ones, to the bowels of the earth,
Pester there the sinners in their agonies;
Flee quickly into dark Acheron,
That is your place, under eternal curse."

49 Thus he speaks, and toward them his heavenly broadsword
Turns, his terrible anger,
For he sees that they are slowly preparing their path,
And do not gladly accept his command.

50 The angelic legion on beautiful, radiant wings
Bravely upon the dark horde struck,
And they recognized from their earlier trial,
That they are invincible with such power.

51 Therefore as a whirlwind they thrash in the sky,
Piercingly, they screech in dark clouds.
Thus squawk crows when an eagle comes between them,
And thus midnight ravens fly in the wind.

52 Only you, Alderan, are their earned prize,
Your soul will be in their victory march,
They snatch this one, from whom flowed so many curses,
Body and spirit he will be their prey.

53 Thus leave the devils the world of light,
And though it still had not dawned,
Yet from delicate, dewy darkness broke
Beautiful dawn, and emboldened all to the good.

54 Zrínyi, knowing well his life's near end,
Counts five hundred brave knights beside him;

As he can no longer bear the burning fire,
He brings these out, with himself.

55 And from the fortress he sallies forth with great, brave heart,
Before him Turks flee in every direction;
In the square he halts, and with harrowing gaze
He looks, to see where are the pagan Turks with great forces.

56 So mercilessly does a lion leave its lair,
And so dreadfully does a comet shine on high:
It does not turn to great nations without destruction,
Horrific fates it carries by its power.

57 Thus do the Turks fear Zrínyi's sight,
For they know, he falls upon them to great harm.
Zrínyi cannot stay in the square because of the fire,
Therefore he slowly strides forth from the outer gate.

58 Where are you now, world-destroying nations?
Where are you, earth-devouring terrible hordes?
Where Turks, where Tatars, where dark Saracens?
Where are you, from three ends of the earth collected
nations?

59 Here stands Zrínyi before you in arms,
Where is the Turkish Mars with rash soul,
Deliman? Where hundreds of others in this horde,
Who thirsted for Zrínyi's blood in peacetime?

60 Courage is sweet on the lips of a man,
But is great and terrible in fatal trial:
This sees, trembling, rash Deliman;
As a summer leaf, so shivers Sultan Suleiman.

61 From a far-off hill he watches Zrínyi's coming out,
But still cannot keep his heart from trembling;

Oh, how often he has regretted his siege of Sziget!
In how many curses has he mired his gray head!

62 But Zrínyi makes no display for the Turks,
He does not tarry showing them
His noble weapons, but goes at them;
Five hundred deaths stride behind his back.

63 Here weapon meets with weapon,
Soldier with soldier is entangled;
Blood, moaning, and dust swirls together heavenward,
Spear, lance, scimitar break, fall apart.

64 In the guise of death the bán walks amongst the Turks,
As the flaming brushfire, when meeting reeds,
As the swift floodwater, when rushing from a mountain;
In such ferocity is Zrínyi bedecked.

65 And falls before him the great giant Chebar,
Yakul dies with a curse, and Chirkin teftedar,[7]
Falls Yakul Baryaktar, green flag and all,
Falls Saracen Zulfikar, of Mahomet's blood.

66 A hundred scimitars, a hundred lances on Zrínyi's shield
Fall decisively, like an avalanche on a house;
But he this cloud, to all's wonder,
Holds back alone, to the destruction of the Turks.

67 But Murtuzan basha, like a wounded bear,
His heart is cooled by shame and vengeance;
He well recalls how, Aigas, bound,
Brought him before Suleiman.[8]

7. A Turkish treasurer.
8. In the earlier Turkish debacle in 4.90–103.

68 But his only son he mourns more:
From Zrínyi's hand was his death.
Therefore to such revenge, deliberately
His heart he has been sharpening to horrific rage.

69 And as a fiery comet[9] he flies down from the clouds,
Whose flaming tail sparks from the roaring fire:
So Murtuzan basha falls upon the Christians,
For death, fury, his heart prepares.

70 He says nothing; terrifyingly,
Bata Péter he fells, dead, before him;
The lives of three Christians he takes away,
And readies for more, is not satisfied yet.

71 He clashes with Novák Iván,
His scimitar meets with his scimitar,
But Novák cuts his hand off with a great blow,
Then his head also, with noble courage.

72 But tarries not here Novákovich Iván,
For by him dies Perviz, Bichir, Arslan;
And no less does Orszics István,
For before him spews forth his spirit: Balbazan.

73 Here start to fall many countless Turks,
Here, every type of pagan is wounded;
Some great Allah, some Mahomet cry,
Lying in their blood and biting the ground.

74 Here flags with flags, in great heaps fall,
There lie many Turks, dead, horses and all,

9. The word here, *liderc,* actually means "incubus," figured here as a demonic comet.

Here half-dead knights collapse on knights;
Under some lie horses, some under horses gasp.

75 Half-dead, a few maul their enemies,
They, as vampires, thirst for blood;
Some release their souls through wounds,
Some, choked by the tumult, leave behind their lives.

76 In heaps lie horses, weapons, and knights;
Christians, also dead, at the great heavens gaze;
But looking toward his soul, at the ground stares the Turk's
Face, for he knows, God shows no mercy.

77 Zrínyi wades horrendously through a lake of blood,
Blood-cataracts he opens in pagans;
From far away recognizes him Deliman,
But his heart trembles, and he is by fear overcome.

78 Never before did he know fear,
But against his will he now trembled,
For he saw Zrínyi's terrible weapon,
Saw his great feats and viciousness.

79 But even through all this his heart stands in place,
When his honor enters his mind,
Many reasons for courage he finds,
And thus, coldly, says to himself:

80 "So am I not now that Deliman,
Who brought harm by his hand into Szigetvár?
He who courageously left in my wake
A lake of blood, a corpse-heap on the Almás-waters' banks?

81 O, my heart: stand forth, my courage!
What do you fear of infidels, my revived pride?

This day and this hour is my entire life,
It is polished by my noble actions.

82 I will go at Zrínyi with my great prowess,
Though he boasts with godly strength;
Us, too, Mahomet aids with great saintliness,
Our bodies, too, are filled with blood.

83 Thus he said and his great spear rattled with his hand,
He builds within his powerful rage;
So in an amphitheatre you may have seen a bull,
Who grinds his horns into the gravel.

84 Who stomps the floor and blows the sand,
Seeing before him his grand foe,
And tries his strength first on a post,
Before turning his weapon against his enemy:

85 Thus does Deliman, and with incredible swiftness
Leaps at the bán, filled with much venom,
Heaves spear at him with mighty strength,
Expects that the great bán will thus die.

86 But the angel of God took his strength,
For on Zrínyi's shield its point went blunt;
The Tatar khan's spear fell to the ground,
Deliman wonders at this occurrence.

87 But with steeled hand he drew his scimitar,
With this to dust the bán's shield wrecked;
But his anger for long could not hold,
For against Zrínyi's sword he could not stand.

88 With vicious blow the bán his helm
Quickly cleaved in two and wounded his neck.

With the other blow he opened his side,
Where he saw a crimson stream copiously flow.

89 The Tatar blows fire, and regathers his strength,
At the bán's chest desperately strikes with his fist,
But the bán cuts the Praecopitan's head in two,
And with his foaming blood, pours out his life.

90 After his death his life flew into darkness,
With great sorrow, as a mist, so vanished;
At the border of death his frenzy subsided,
And his soul into eternal night with many others dissolved.

91 And nothing does Zrínyi tarry at his death,
But more and more he sacrifices, and into a great pile
heaves;
Little fuel for such a blaze are three hundred pagans,
These cuts down the Croat bán.

92 But immediately when fell the brave Deliman,
The entire Turkish camp quickly terrified.
The most courageous men begin to tremble,
And then flee, as they have strength.

93 With the fleeing hordes he mingled,
Strikes everywhere at the fleeing hordes.
Finally even to the emperor drew near,
Even from afar Zrínyi recognized him.

94 And one great plea to God he surrenders,
For his nobility's test he seeks;
Then swiftly he charges, there where he saw the emperor,
In his sword carries his terrible thunder.

95 Many thousand bostandjis, countless spahoglans,
The terrified emperor surround as a mountain;

But through all those lunges the Croatian bán,
Makes a path by his horrific strength.

96 For no one dares stand before him,
No one dares look into his valiant eyes;
A hundred at once he kills in one place,
And unto another hundred brings merciless death.

97 Suleiman to mount his good horse quickly hurries,
But the bán's speed had long brought him there,
Ten of the emperor's aides he cuts down there,
And then to emperor Zrínyi thus began:

98 "Bloodsucking selendek,[10] despoiler of the world,
The hour of your greed has come;
God your sins no longer pardons,
You must depart, ancient cur, to eternal damnation."

99 Thus saying, at his waist he splits him in two,
His blood and his life he spills onto the earth;
Cursing, the emperor releases his soul,
Which his body held so proudly in life.

100 This was the end of great emperor Suleiman,
This, of his great renowned power;
God allowed Count Zrínyi Miklós
The glory of this extraordinary trial.

101 Then the bán looks back, sees from afar:
His stranded army falls by Turks' swords;
As a shepherd to his flock, he quickly turns,
And calls to them thus in loud voice:

10. A Croatian word for a hunting dog.

102 “Thus long we have lived, soldiers, for the glory of
Him, who died on a cross for our freedom:
Let us die happily today, and for our good names
Let us therefore die courageously.

103 There I see the kingdom of God opened up,
There I recognize well Elohim’s son!
I see, I see, the angel of God:
Of enduring branches, he holds for us a crown.”

104 But countless Turks surround the army,
From afar the janissaries fire at the knights,
For they dare not test them by the sword;
No one dares await their hands.

105 Through all this there is not one cry,
For with great joy and gladness all die.
Those who stand in place, at that same spot
Give their souls over to God.

106 Near the great bán no one dares go,
But janissary missiles throw Zrínyi to the ground:
Into his chest one lodged, another his forehead strikes,
Together with his men, lays him on the ground.

107 The angelic legion immediately descends,
Glorifying God with ringing music.
Gabriel with twice ten others, the bán’s soul
Lifts from the ground on splendid wings.

108 And every angel carries a soul,
Before God thus carry these.
The whole angelic corps magnificent harmony began,
And left it unto me, my words to end.

God of knights, verily your servant
Did not pity from you his worldly ruin;
By his blood formed great words,
With such signature gave himself to you;
For his noble blood, have favor on his son.[11]

11. I.e., his great-grandson, the author.

POSTSCRIPT

1 Here I have brought my work to a close,
Which jealous time nor water can wash away,
Nor the heavens' thunder nor iron can ruin,
Nor that great enemy, jealousy, can harm.

2 And when that day comes, which over my body
Alone can triumph, let on my life be expended
Its power: my greater portion indeed
Is carried on the wind to the high heavens.

3 And from Scythia, wherefrom came the Magyar warrior,
Whose heroism the world saw, great regions of it,
From those places all eyes look on me,
With fame and respect, as long as the world is.

4 But my fame I do not gain by my pen alone,
But with my terrible pain-bringing scimitar:
As long as I live, I strive with the Ottoman horde,
Happily blanket my homeland with its ashes.

EPIGRAMS

The following short verses, taken from a series of six, were penned by the author separately from the prior text.

ZRÍNYI MIKLÓS OF SZIGET

As Hector to Troy,
So I to Szigetvár
Stalwart defender was;

I showed the pagans,
That to great Jehovah
Beloved servant I was,

And sooner my life,
Rather than my devotion,
From my body I released.

DELI VID SARKOVICS

I, too, not a little
Accomplished, to make fall
The world-destroying pagan curs;

A great dent made I
In the Ottoman crescent:
There will be none more diligent;

For my lord, my homeland,
For great God's son
My life was the least I could give.

VAJDAS RADIVOJ AND JURANICS

We were happy;
Together we lived, died,
Now our souls are with God;

At great Zrínyi's side
Our fame swelled,
For him we suffered death:

But it was not in vain,
Because his good grandson
Made us immortal.

FARKASICS PÉTER

Barely showed,
Then snatched me away
Did cruel fate;

My good lord mourned me,
And his son wrote well of me,
Therefore my fame is assured.

Not everything is meant to be
In the life of every man;
May God's will so be done.

GLOSSARY OF TURKISH, CROATIAN, AND HUNGARIAN WORDS

aga: a title of rank of the Ottoman Empire, denoting military or political power, akin to "governor" or "general."

basha: a title of rank of the Ottoman Empire, denoting military or political power, akin to "governor" or "general."

bán: a title of nobility, equivalent to "count"; from the Slavic "master" or "lord."

bég: a title of rank of the Ottoman Empire, denoting military or political power, akin to "governor" or "general."

beglerbég: a title of rank, superior to bég.

bostandji: an imperial bodyguard.

chausse: a Turkish courier.

dervish: actually a member of the mystical Sufi sect of Islam; was often used by Christian writers to mean any Muslim soldier.

dolman: a part of the Ottoman military uniform, a long, capelike garment with sleeves.

hodja: a muezzin; criers who call the faithful to their daily prayers.

janissary: elite Ottoman infantrymen, raised as soldiers from childhood, and often recruited from orphanages and conquered peoples; famed for their skill with muskets.

kadia: a Turkish judge.

kajmekan: a Turkish word indicating a person chosen to represent the office or views of another, particularly the sultan.

kapidji-basha: chief sergeant-at-arms.

khan: a title of royalty originating from central Asia, especially favored by the Mongols and Tatars.

Magyars: the Hungarian ethnic group or nation.

oda-basha: a title of rank, superior to *basha.*

olay-bég: a title of rank, superior to *bég.*

padishah: a title of royalty, literally "high king." Though *basha* actually originated as a contraction of it, *padishah,* when used as such, was exclusive to sultans.

Pannonia: Roman province comprising the Carpathian Basin, which includes Hungary and Croatia, among others.

sanjay: a class of Ottoman infantry.

selendek: a Croatian word for a hunting dog.

spahoglan: regular Ottoman cavalry.

talisman: a Turkish cleric.

teftedar: a Turkish treasurer.

timar: a title of rank, less prestigious than *bég.*

vajda: a title of nobility, equivalent to "duke"; from the Slavic "war-leader."

LIST OF CHARACTERS

Descriptions are followed by first mention in text.

THE DEFENDERS OF SZIGETVÁR

Alapi Gáspár: commander, Zrínyi's nephew, who wears a panther pelt (5.48).

Balázs: commander and scribe (5.54).

Barbála: Deli Vid's wife, a Turk of Berber ancestry (13.6).

Bata Péter: commander (5.52).

Bika András: commander, whose name means "bull"; friend of Medvei Benedek (5.54).

Cserei Pál: commander, friend of Kobács Miklós, killed in the Battle of Siklós Plain (3.92).

Dandó: commander (5.45).

Deli Vid: commander, Zrínyi's chief warrior. Has nearly unparalleled strength and wields a four-fathom lance (24 feet). Married to the faithful Barbála, a Turk.

Farkasics Péter: two different characters, both commanders under Zrínyi, whom the author confounds. Despite language indicating that this is one man who is wounded, recovers, and then relapses, other sources indicate that they are, in fact, two individuals. The first appears at 3.67, where he suffers a mortal blow, from which he later dies. The second make his only appearance at 5.39 to take the oath with the defenders.

Geréci Berta: commander, who was wounded and lost much of his unit in the Battle of Siklós Plain (5.55).

Guszics András: commander, who had previously defended Fort Zrin, the Zrínyi family's castle, against Ottoman attack (5.58).

Győri Mátyás: commander (5.54).

Juranics: commander, recently promoted after his commander's death. Best friend of the more experienced Radivoj, with whom he undertakes an espionage mission in 9.56.

Kobács Miklós: commander (5.53).

Medvei Benedek: commander, whose name means "bear"; friend of Bika András (5.54).

Novákovics Iván: commander, who wears a tiger pelt (5.43).

Orostoni Péter: commander (5.57).

Orsics István: commander (5.45).

Radivoj: commander, also known as "Horvát Radivoj" (Croatian Radivoj), best friend of the relatively inexperienced Juranics, with whom he undertakes an espionage mission in part 9 (5.58).

Stipán Golemi: commander (5.51).

Szecsődi Máté: commander (5.47).

Zrínyi György: Zrínyi Miklós' son, and grandfather of the author. Still a youth at the time of the siege, he is sent by his father to the safety of the emperor's court (2.86).

Zrínyi Miklós: count, devout leader of the defenders of Szigetvár. Lived 1508–1566, and was 58 at the time of the Siege of Sziget. The author's great grandfather (2.60).

THE OTTOMAN FORCES

Aigas: Mameluke general, captain of the sultan's guard (1.89).

Alderan: Saracen general, quartermaster, and wizard, famed for his exceptional intellect and skill at necromancy; brother of Demirham (1.84).

Ali Kurtog: Beglerbég of Asia, and master of artillery for the Ottoman forces (6.54).

Amirassen: Saracen general, owner of the famed horse Karabul (1.79).

Arslan: incompetent *bég* of Budapest, an alcoholic and opium addict (1.61).

Cumilla: Sultan Suleiman's beautiful daughter, married to Rushtan, whom she detests (1.71).

Deliman: Tatar khan, one of the sultan's chief warriors, young and hotheaded. In love with Cumilla, the sultan's daughter, who is married to Rushtan (1.69).

Demirham: Saracen general, famed for his inhuman strength; brother of Alderan (1.82).

Halul: prestigious Ottoman diplomat, sent to Szigetvár to fulfill the formality of asking for surrender (6.2).

Hamvivan: inexperienced son of King Menetham of Syria, placed in the charge of his bodyguard, Kamber (1.82).

Ibrahim (*olay-bég*): ruthless but wise Ottoman governor of Pécs, some 30 kilometers from Szigetvár (2.86).

Kadilesker: supreme Ottoman cleric, his position comparable to "high priest" and "archbishop," as he is referred to by Zrínyi (4.66).

Mehmet Guylirgi: also known as Tayeleri Mehmet, Rash and naive Ottoman governor of Bosnia, who tries to camp under Szigetvár without worrying about Christian attacks; father of Rézmán (2.8).

Osman: infantry commander for the Ottoman forces (6.53).

Petraf: beglerbég of Greece, who asked for and received the surrender of Kerecseni László at Gyula, who he then treacherously took captive (2.52).

Radován Andrián: a *vajda* of Croatia and close friend of Zrínyi's, captured by the Ottomans sometime before the siege, and ransomed by Zrínyi in exchange for Ibrahim (2.49).

Rushtan: one of the sultan's top generals and advisors, married to Cumilla, the sultan's daughter (1.73).

Sokolovich Mehmet: best known today as Sokollu Mehmed, an extremely trusted advisor to the sultan. Would serve in the same capacity to the next two Ottoman sultans as well, eventually becoming the de facto ruler behind the throne for some years before being assassinated (4.66).

Sultan Suleiman: known as "the Magnificent," lived 1494–1566 and became sultan of the Ottoman Empire in 1520. Considered by the author to be one of the wisest rulers in all the world, but marred by a streak of ruthlessness. Personally led the Ottoman forces in the Siege of Sziget.

BIBLIOGRAPHY

prepared by Steven Béla Várdy

Ágoston, Gábor. "Az Iszlám erős védőgátja: Az oszmán hódítás és a magyarországi oszmán végvidék" [The strong defensive rampart of Islam: The Ottoman Conquest and the Ottoman frontier in Hungary], in *A magyar hadtörténelem évszázadai* [Centuries of Hungarian military history], edited by Béla K. Király and László Veszprémy (Budapest: Atlanti Kutató és Kiadó Közalapítvány, 2003), 61–76. (Hereafter: *A magyar hadtörténelem évszázadai.*)

———. "Ottoman Conquest and the Ottoman Military Frontier in Hungary," in *A Millennium of Hungarian Military History*, edited by Béla Király and László Veszprémy. New York: Atlantic Research and Publications, 2002.

———. "The Ottoman-Habsburg Frontier in Hungary, 1541–1699: A Comparison." In *The Great Ottoman, Turkish Civilization,* edited by Güler Eren et al., 4 vols. Ankara: Yeni Türkiye Dergisi, 2000, 276–87. (Hereafter: *The Great Ottoman, Turkish Civilization.*)

Alföldi, László M. "The Battle of Mohács, 1526. " In *From Hunyadi to Rákóczi: War and Society in Late Medieval and Early Modern Hungary,* edited by János M. Bak and Béla K. Király . New York: Social Sciences Monographs, East European Monographs, Distributed by Columbia University Press, 1982, 189–202. (Hereafter: *From Hunyadi to Rákóczi.*)

A magyar hadtörténelem évszázadai [Centuries of Hungarian military history]. Edited by Béla K. Király and László Veszprémy. Budapest: Atlanti Kutató és Kiadó Közalapítvány, 2003.

Bán, Imre. "Zrínyi Miklós" [Miklós Zrínyi], in *Magyar irodalom története 1600-tól 1772-ig* [History of Hungarian literature from 1600 to 1772], edited by Tibor Klaniczay. Budapest: Akadémiai Kiadó, 1964, 159–84.

Bayerle, Gustav. "One Hundred Fifty Years of Frontier Life in Hungary." In *From Hunyadi to Rákóczi*, 227–42.

Benda, Kálmán. "Zrínyi Miklós, a Szigetvári hős" [Miklós Zrínyi, the hero of Szigetvár], in *Szigetvári Emlékkönyv. Szigetvár 1566. évi ostromának 400. évfordulójára* [Szigetvár memorial volume: On the 400th anniversary of the siege of Szigetvár], edited by Lajos Rúzsás. Budapest: Akadémiai Kiadó, 1966, 15–37. (Hereafter: *Szigetvári Emlékkönyv.*)

Bende, Lajos. "Sziget ostroma 1566-ban" [The siege of Sziget in 1566]. In *Szigetvári Emlékkönyv*, 61–104.

Benedek, Elek. *Szigeti veszedelem. Gróf Zrínyi Miklós költeménye nyomán írta Benedek Elek* [Peril of Sziget]. Written by Elek Benedek on the Basis of the Epic by Count Miklós Zrínyi. Budapest: Lamper R. & Wodianer F. és Fiai, 1914.

Brodarics históriája a mohácsi vészől [Brodarics's history about the battle of Mohács]. Translated by Imre Szentpétery. Budapest: Lampel Róbert-Wodainer F. és Fia, reprinted by Zrínyi Katonai Kiadó, 1977.

Budina Sámuel históriája magyarul és latinul Szigetvár 1566. évi ostromáról [Sámuel Budina's history in Hungarian and in Latin about the siege of Szigetvár in 1566]. Szigetvár: A Szigetvári Várbaráti Kör Kiadványai, 1978.

Csuday, Jenő. *Zrínyiek a magyar történelemben, 1566–1704* [The Zrínyis in Hungarian history]. Szombathely, Hungary: Seiler Henrikné Kiadása, 1884.

Domonkos, Leslie S. "The Battle of Mohács as a Cultural Watershed." In *From Hunyadi to Rákóczi*, 203–24.

Evlia Cselebi török világutazó magyarországi utazásai, 1660–1664 [Turkish World traveler Evliya Chelebi's travels in Hungary, 1660–1664]. 2nd ed. Budapest: Gondolat Kiadó, 1985.

From Hunyadi to Rákóczi: War and Society in Late Medieval and Early Modern Hungary. Edited by János M. Bak and Béla K. Király. New York: Social Sciences Monographs, East European Monographs, distributed by Columbia University Press, 1982.

Gökbilgin, Tayyib. "Nagy Szolimán 1566. évi szigetvár elleni hadjáratának előzményei" [Events preceding Süleyman the Great's campaign against Szigetvár in 1566]. In *Szigetvári Emlékkönyv*, 53–59.

The Great Ottoman, Turkish Civilization. Edited by Güler Eren et al. 4 vols. Ankara: Yeni Türkiye Dergisi, 2000.

Hegyi, Klára. "The Ottoman Network of Fortresses in Hungary." In *Ottomans, Hungarians, and Habsburgs in Central Europe: The Military Confines in the Era of Ottoman Conquest*, edited by Géza Dávid and Pál Fodor. Leiden and Boston: Brill Academic Publishers, 2000, 163–93.

Hegyi, Klára, and Vera Zimányi. *The Ottoman Empire in Europe.* Budapest: Corvina Kiadó, 1986.

Hess, Andrew C. "The Road to Victory: The Significance of Mohács for Ottoman Expansion." In *From Hunyadi to Rákóczi,* 179–88.

Klaniczay, Tibor. *Zrínyi Miklós* [Miklós Zrínyi]. Budapest: Akadémiai Kiadó, 1954.

Kubinyi, András. "The Road to Defeat: Hungarian Politics and Defense in the Jagellonian Period." In *From Hunyadi to Rákóczi,* 159–78.

Maksay, Ferenc. "Peasantry and Mercenary Service in Sixteenth-Century Hungary." In *From Hunyadi to Rákóczi,* 261–74.

Nagy, Iván. *Magyarország családai czímerekkel és nemzedékrendi táblákkal* [Hungary's families with coats of arms and genealogical tables], 12 vols. and one supplement. Pest, 1857–1868), 12.435–42.

Pálffy, Géza. "A törökellenes határvédelmi rendszer a 16–17. században" [The anti-Turkish system of defense in the 16th and 17th centuries]. In *A magyar hadtörténelem évszázadai,* 77–92.

Perjés, Géza. "Gróf Zrínyi Miklós, 1620–1664" [Count Miklós Zrínyi, 1620–1664]. In *A magyar hadtörténelem évszázadai,* 109–22.

———. *Zrínyi Miklós és Kora* [Miklós Zrínyi and his age]. Budapest: Akadémiai Kiadó, 1965.

———. "The Zrínyi-Montecuccoli Controversy." In *From Hunyadi to Rákóczi,* 335–50.

Preveden, Francis R. *A History of the Croatian People.* 2 vols. New York: Philosophical Library, 1955–1962.

Prpic, George J. *Croatia and Hungary during the Turkish Era.* Cleveland, Ohio: Center for Southern-Hungarian and Balkan Studies, 1973. (A special issue of the *Awakener.*)

Régi magyar levelestár [Collection of old Hungarian letters]. 2 vols. Budapest: Magvető Kiadó, 1981. (This collection has dozens of letters by both the older and the younger Nicholas Zrínyi.)

Rothenberg, Gunther Erich. *The Austrian Military Border in Croatia, 1522–1747.* Urbana, Ill.: Illinois Studies in Social Sciences, 1960.

Rúzsás, Lajos. "The Siege of Szigetvár of 1566: Its Significance in Hungarian Social Development." In *From Hunyadi to Rákóczi,* 251–74.

Salamon, Ferencz. *Az első Zrínyiek* [The early Zrínyis]. Pest: Hekenast Gusztáv, 1865.

———. *Magyarország a török hódítás korában* [Hungary in the period of Turkish conquest]. 2nd ed. Budapest: Franklin-Társulat, 1885.

Salamon, Franz. *Ungarn im Zeitalter der Türkenherrschaft* [Hungary in the period of Turkish conquest]. Translated from Hungarian by Gustav Jurány. Leipzig: H. Haessel Verlag, 1887.

Süleyman the Magnificent and His Age. Edited by Metin Kunt and Christine Woodhead. London: Longman Publishers, 1995.

Szakály, Ferenc. "The Hungarian-Croatian Border Defense System and Its Collapse." In *From Hunyadi to Rákóczi,* 141–58.

Szántó, Imre. *A végvári rendszer és fénykora Magyarországon, 1541–1593* [The frontier fortress system and its climax in Hungary, 1541–1593]. Budapest: Akadémiai Kiadó, 1980.

Szelaniki Musztafa leírása Szigetvár ostromáról [Mustafa Szelaniki's description of the siege of Szigetvár]. Szigetvár: A Szigetvári Várbaráti Kör Kiadványai, 1979.

Szigetvár eleste 1566-ban és visszafoglalása 1689-ben, egykor leírások alapján [The fall of Szigetvár in 1566 and its reconquest in 1689, based on contemporary accounts]. Edited by Imre Molnár. Szigetvár: A Szigetvári Várbaráti Kör Kiadványai, 1980.

Szigetvári Emlékkönyv. Szigetvár 1566. évi ostromának 400. évfordulójára [Szigetvár memorial volume: On the 400th anniversary of the siege of Szigetvár]. Edited by Lajos Rúzsás. Budapest: Akadémiai Kiadó, 1966. (Hereafter: *Szigetvári Emlékkönyv.*)

Takáts, Sándor. *A török hódoltság korából* [From the period of the Turkish conquest]. Budapest: Genius Kiadás, 1928.

———. "A Zrínyiek magyarsága" [The Hungarian identity of the Zrínyis]. In Sándor Takáts, *Magyar küzdelmek* [Hungarian struggles]. Budapest: Genius Kiadás, 1929, 41–53. (Hereafter: Takáts, *Magyar küzdelmek.*)

———. *Rajzok a török világból* [Sketches from the Turkish world]. 3 vols. Budapest: Magyar Tudományos Akadémia Kiadása, 1915–1917.

———. "Zrínyi-levelek" [Zrínyi letters]. In Takáts, *Magyar küzdelmek,* 105–81.

———. "Zrínyi Miklós emlékezete" [Remembering Miklós Zrínyi]. In Sándor Takáts, *Bajvívó magyarok* [Dueling Hungarians], 3rd ed. (Budapest: Móra Könyvkiadó, 1979), 273–86.

———. "Zrínyi Miklós temetése" [Miklós Zrínyi's funeral]. In Sándor Takáts, *Régi idők, régi emberek* [Times of old, people of old], 2nd ed. Budapest: Athenaeum Irodalmi és Nyomdai R.T., 1922, 113–23.

Tóth, István. "A szigeti hős alakja a magyar irodalomban" [The image of the hero of Sziget in Hungarian literature]. In *Szigetvári Emlékkönyv,* 307–47.

Waczulik, Margit. "Szigetvár 1566. évi ostroma az egykorú történetírásban" [The siege of Szigetvár in contemporary historical writings]. In *Szigetvári Emlékkönyv,* 287–306.

Zrínyi Miklós a szigetvári hős életére vonatkozó levelek és okiratok [Letters and documents relating to the life of Miklós Zrínyi, the hero of Szigetvár]. Edited by Samu Barabás, 2 vols. Budapest: Monumenta Hungariae Historica, 1898–1899.

Zrínyi Miklós haditudományi munkái [Miklós Zrínyi's work on warfare]. Introduced by László Benczédi and Géza Perjés. Budapest: Zrínyi Kiadó, 1957.

The Siege of Sziget was designed and typeset in Minion by Kachergis Book Design of Pittsboro, North Carolina. It was printed on 55-pound Natural and bound by Versa Press of East Peoria, Illinois.